Praise for *Courtship, The Lost Art*

Your work is so thoughtful and synthetic; you pull from several traditions to give the reader a large panoramic sense of love. I like the particularity of dream, fantasy, and reverie throughout. Dennis Slattery, Ph.D., author of *Simon's Crossing*.

You are an original thinker and writer and have added an important perspective to the subject of love in today's conversation. Every chapter was full of interest, knowledge, and wonderful insights about aspects of love. I am very impressed by the breadth and depth you brought to the subject. When finishing I felt like I had gone on a personal odyssey and I thank you for that. Taj Inayat, MA, Vice President, Sufi Order International.

After reading the book I am able to locate my own experience. I reflect differently on what has been and yet to be. I guess you could say the book gave me a new sight, naïveté is over and done... the author left me knowing a lot! In the end I believe any who read it will view with newness what love is and what it can be if we have a bit of courage. Wendy Tremayne, author and event producer.

Courtship, the Lost Art

Where is Love in the Twenty-First Century?

MaryRose Bennett, Ph.D.

Axis Mundi Publications

Albuquerque, New Mexico

Published by Axis Mundi Publications.

Printed in the United States by Lightning Source Inc.

Book Design and Editing by Ahad Cobb
Borders and Ornaments by Robert Powers
Front Cover Photograph by Thea Witt
Back Cover Photograph by Ahad Cobb

MaryRose Bennett's website is
consciousnesscounselingeducation.com

Library of Congress Control Number: 2011903963
ISBN: 978-0-7875-9963-8

Dedication:

To my patients, who are a constant source of inspiration,
who are the heart and soul of a new consciousness…
to the ecstatic dancers on the path of love…
to friends and lovers in the world…
and to my beloved One….
Without all of you this book would not have been possible!

Acknowledgement

Ahad,
I want to thank you for dreaming this dream forward with me…
for your constant enthusiasm, support, and vision…
for the endless hours you dedicated
to the editing, layout, and design of this book…
for the love, harmony, and beauty you have brought to this prayer…
for the song you have sung…
Only Love,
Widad

Table of Contents

Introduction

The inception of this book is one of radical grace, radical in the sense that it liberates the mind and frees the soul to experience Love. This book speaks to a growing "quiet minority" who are becoming the new majority, the avant garde, the new consciousness, the emergent paradigm pulsing in the heartbeat of humanity.

Courtship, The Lost Art is a gentle, respectful, passionate rhapsody and probing inquiry, approaching the presence of love from many perspectives. Each perception, each sensation, each emotion we have about love is true, yet love itself is greater than any of our approaches to her. Love itself is our guide.

What soul wants most is to be heard, to be seen, to be visible, to experience reflections of love. Courtship is a process which reflects, enhances, and affirms the inner life, a form of relating erotically in a symbolic way between the courtier and the lady. The maidens of the regal court are conscious of the interplay between Eros and Spirit. They are imbued with divine graces. They recognize this in themselves, which makes them ultimately attractive to the onlookers of the court, the felt experience of impossible love, untouchable love, and unattainable love. The love she occupies is divine love.

This is an exploratory conversation based on experience, scholarship, and reflection. We will survey the medieval model of courtly love and contemporary depth perspectives; the role our personal mythologies have in shaping our experience, and the dark shadows of love; the myth of soul mates, the myth that splits; our sexual history and sacred sexuality; the sociology, biology, and chemistry of love; alternative models of relationship emerging in present time; the alchemy of love, the turn to the inner life, and the path of the mystic. And yet love itself is greater still than all our explorations.

Chapter Summaries

Chapter One: Courtly Love

Courtly love is the contemplation of the divine ideal in human form, the adoration of the beauty, virtue, and intelligence of the beloved. The ennobling quality of love between the courtier and the longed-for lady or "Mystical Queen" elevates and blesses them into a deeper, greater union. Courtship is erotic spirituality embodied in the heart of human longing for the Divine, the Holy Other. The courtship between two lovers forms a container for the activity of the sacred, the Beloved. Contemporary relationships are in chaos due to the loss of love as a spiritual experience. The intent of this book is to address the ever-present human longing for love. Our goal is to return to courtship, to the sacred, to love as a spiritual path.

Chapter Two: Personal Mythology

There are many encounters that influence how we define the love experience. Our personal myth is the story we tell ourselves or have been told about who we are, our worth and value. Personal myths not only influence and shape our personality but can also define our love experiences. Unresolved wounds and repressed emotional pain constellate the human shadow and take the seeker into the realm of the dark erotic, attracting archetypal encounters in the guise of true lovers. A love affair devoid of courtship results in a rapid fall into love. When lovers fall into love without establishing trust, couples are vulnerable to suffering and have a tendency to enact relentless psychodramas. Dark Eros is chaotic, with no love and no connection. Passionate love has been characterized as dramatic, obsessive, and potentially violent — although passion itself is not violent. However, romantic passion in courtship is experienced as a natural flow of mutual love, respect, and consideration, a

3

balance between stability and passionate depths. These encounters strip us of our naïvetè and propel us into the depths, only to bring to light that which has been unconscious. We are invited to dispel the myth, re-write the story, and redefine love from a fresh awareness.

Chapter Three: Soul Mates

Plato suggests that, due to the hubris of humanity toward God, humans who were once complete and whole are now divided in half. Consequently, humans spend a great deal of their life seeking their "other half." The myth of soul mates splits and divides human beings, producing fragmentation in both the personal and collective psyche. Divisions produce cultural symptoms which include gender differentiation, disassociation from the body, depression, loneliness, alienation, and melancholia. To repair the split we need to move away from fragmentation towards cohesion and discover that each soul is whole and complete, as well as individual and unique. Our growth to wholeness within us and in relationship to others involves accepting and nurturing our own androgynous and genderfluid nature.

Chapter Four: Sexual History

Only half of humanity carries a genetic predisposition to remain married and faithful, while the other half is a unique potpourri of coupling dispositions, spreading and enhancing those genes. Extra-marital affairs, trysts, and "special friends" are the result of ancient reproductive strategy used by both sexes. We carry forth the genetic blueprint and brain chemistry for marriage, divorce, and remarriage, also referred to as serial monogamy, the most common love style in the U.S. today. In a rapidly changing world, we are seeking a coupling that is compatible with our ancient human spirit yet does not preclude sacred sexuality. Sacred sex shifts the emphasis from procreation to sacred ecstasy. Sacred sex is a vehicle for conscious co-creation and union with the Divine in each of us and through one another.

Chapter Five: The Biology and Chemistry of Love

In our world today there are couples who benefit from a traditional marriage model. Yet for others the traditional models of relationship do not work. Anthropologist Desmond Morris provides a well-researched framework for those seeking a pair-bonded experience, and addresses the biology of love. Dr. Helen Fisher, a biological anthropologist, gives an illuminating perspective on the power and paradoxes of human sexuality. Her revolutionary work on "the brain chemistry of love" provides answers for those who don't adapt to a traditional model. For instance, one person can be biologically capable of being stabilized in marriage with one person while being totally in love with another person while at the same time having sex with whoever is available at the moment, and/or experiencing all three love activities with the same person.

Chapter Six: Love in the Twenty-First Century: Alternative Models and Trends

When we look at marriage today in America, we find we are moving from the traditional "gender role marriage" to the "companionate marriage." We hold two values at once: a culture of marriage and a culture of individualism. Medieval courtly love can be seen as an origin of the modern notion of the personal self. Romantic love cultivates interdependence, experienced as the interchange between love and freedom, union and autonomy. Alternative models involve imagining realties together, realities which are soul-making rather than soul-taking. New trends include the invitation to the sacred marriage, a true monogamy centered on the One Divinity in humanity.

Chapter Seven: Love and the Erotic Pulse

The alchemical journey between Sol and Luna is a story about the realization of love. Sol (Sun) and Luna (Moon) represent the archetypal masculine and feminine principles of our inner being. Love is the cosmic chemical which summons each toward the other. At each stage of the alchemical courtship the union is refined and purified. Each chemical operation brings the other closer to the embodiment of heaven here on earth.

Chapter Eight: The Inner Turn: The Eternal Courtship

There comes a time on the path of love when the external world no longer satisfies our needs. Endless, senseless, looking and seeking is accompanied by fear, anxiety, frustration and disappointment. There is a constant longing and desire for something greater, which is difficult to describe or define. This is the time for the inner turn. One turns within to discover, listen, learn, and evolve. The inner turn is a spiritual passage into conscious relationship with the Divine. Meditation is the bridge to the inner world, met by the depth perspective, which awakens us to love by attending to metaphors, sensing, listening, hearing, and engaging our dreams. We recognize that we are connected to all of creation. The divine mystery seeks to reveal itself through you, through her, through him, by drawing forward what is hidden in our souls.

Chapter Nine: The Path of the Mystic

The art of courtship has its roots in mystical tradition. The comprehension of the Divine is attained through direct experience, fostered by sensing, personal insight, and self-knowledge. Courtship with the Beloved occurs when the inner life and the spiritual life merge. The inner turn converges with the mystical path. Spousal mystics approached the divine with a devotional attitude and commitment to embody spiritual tenets. Spousal mystics partake in a dialogic communion to access the depths. Knowing God as Love, Lover, and Beloved, opens oneself wholly and completely to the Divine. God is felt as a deep unity and love for all of humanity.

Gender and Capitalization

God is beyond gender, beyond "he" or "she" or "it." Although God may occasionally be referred to as *Him* or *Her* in this text, this is for convenience only and not meant to define or delimit God in any way. Likewise, God may be referred to as *the Divine, the Beloved, the Source,* to name a few; these terms are indicative but not in any way definitive. Although we can apprehend the presence of God in life and in form, the essence of God is beyond classification, indeed beyond human comprehension.

You will notice that certain words in this text are capitalized in one context but not capitalized in other contexts, specifically *self* and *Self, beloved* and *Beloved, other* and *Other*. When the word is capitalized it refers to the divine, total aspect of the concept, and when it is not capitalized it refers to the human, individualized aspect of the concept. For instance, *self* refers to the ego whereas *Self* refers to the whole and complete being, which includes but is much greater than the ego.

There is a certain ambiguity, however, in this distinction, and it is not always clear whether Beloved, for instance, should be capitalized or not. The divine and the human dimensions of reality are not separate from each other, but rather exist along a continuum. When love opens our heart we can see the Divine Beloved present in the human beloved and the Holy Other present in another human being.

Chapter One
Courtly Love

Many lovers are called to experience relationship as a path of awakening. Others experience sacred love as an invitation and for others love itself is lived as a spiritual experience. Hearts are harkened in a variety of ways: through a personal dream, through a spiritual vision, through the agony and heartbreak of a relationship. And no doubt many a heart has been awakened by a love song, a sonnet, or the depth of vast silence. The lover is summoned and turns her heart towards the Beloved. The journey of courtship begins.

We begin our conversation about courtship with a brief contemplation of courtly love. The tradition of courtly love arose in the courts of Southern France in the eleventh century and spread north throughout Europe, becoming an essential element of the chivalric tradition of the knights, which was celebrated in the great medieval romances. Courtly love begins with the lover seeing divine beauty, wisdom, and virtue embodied in the presence of the beloved. Courtly love promotes a dynamic tension between sexual attraction and spiritual aspiration as a path for the ennoblement of the soul.

Courtly love was the first time the practice of spiritual love between men and women, outside of marriage, apart from sex, emerged in Western culture after the Dark Ages. Courtly love is a relevant starting point in our conversation about seeking a higher love than is embodied in both conventional marriage standards and our hypersexual pop culture. Courtly love takes the mutual attraction between a man and a woman as a path to elevate the soul through sublimated desire and refined behavior.

The image we have of the troubadour is that of the courtier standing under the balcony of the lady he is wooing, holding a lute and singing to her of the love he has for her beauty and virtue. We think of troubadours as wandering minstrels, and no doubt wandering minstrels brought Sufi love songs from Andalusia into southern France. The actual troubadours whose poetry survives were mostly the highly educated lords and ladies of the courts, whereas the jongleurs were the musicians who performed their compositions publicly.

The lady is married, of higher caste, sexually and socially unavailable, typically the high-born lady of the castle. She can also be the *princesse lointaine*, the far-away princess, physically distant. The courtier holds her image in his heart and devotes his love to her. This love is elevating, as contrasted with socially arranged marriages. Although the troubadours were mostly male, there were women *trobairitz* who expressed love for men in a similar way. The *trobairitz* sang the ideals of perfect love reflected in their personal experience, as well as love for women.

This idealized love of elevated ladies is incorporated in the codes of chivalry, in which the knight pledges himself to protect and defend (and rescue, if necessary) his lady without expecting much more than her compassionate glance and gratitude in return. At first this was a secret romantic love, where the lovers would steal away to be alone together. As time went on and courtly love became more popular, their behavior was guided by elaborate codes of etiquette and their love affairs became a quasi-public phenomenon. The lover would wear his beloved's colors and declare his love in song, referring to his beloved only by a symbolic name, such as "Precious Rose."

Not only nobility of spirit but ultimately spiritual redemption is won from devotion to the beloved, who greets the lover after death with a salute and a kiss, welcoming him to heaven. Salvation, formerly possessed solely by the church, now comes from the favor of the beloved. The reward is the opening of the heart to Love itself. Dante Alighieri, author of *The Divine Comedy*, saw his beloved Beatrice only three times in his earthly life, beholding her from a distance, and yet in his imagination she became his guide through the angelic realms of paradise. Dante was one of the *Fideli de Amore*, the Faithful Lovers, a group of poets who engaged in an erotic spirituality that sought nobility through personal virtue rather than inherited status.

Courtly love (*l'amour courtois*) is an idealistic love, the contemplation of the divine ideal in human form, the adoration of and devotion to her beauty, virtue, and intelligence. Love of the beloved expands the capacity of the heart of the lover, and both are drawn closer to divine love through this courtship, through love itself, *fin amour* (fine love). Courtly love was essentially a path to divine union, although it certainly had more mundane goals as well. The troubadours sought recognition and acclaim, not to mention sexual favors, just as contemporary singer-songwriters do. The troubadours were, after all, entertainers, promoting a reputation of being crazy for love, and often making fools of themselves for love.

The pathos, the longing, and the ennobling quality of courtly love is no less real for being ideal, especially as it elevates the vision of the beloved woman from that of personal property and sex object to a divine vision. This ennobling quality of love works both ways; it elevates and blesses both he/she who gives and she/he who receives. For the evocation (calling forth) of the beloved is also the education (drawing forth) of the soul qualities of the beloved. We discover our Selves in loving and in being loved.

Food Court at the Airport

At the beginning of writing this book, a collective dream was presented:

"I have flown into New York and am waiting for the plane that will take me home. I check in my bags and then have several hours to wait for the flight. I am sitting at a food court. A couple sitting across the food court (a rectangle of tables around an empty space) catches my attention. He is a tall, lanky, unshaven young man in a dark trench coat, i.e. a poet type, my shadow figure. She is tall, slender, pale, Gaelic, with long strawberry blonde hair. He prods her and prompts her until she begins singing the songs of the faeries. Her voice is soft and yet penetrates the deepest layers of my being. Her voice is like the wind blowing, sussurating through the birch trees, stripping the leaves away on a beautiful fall day. Her songs are incomprehensible and yet speak directly to my soul. I begin weeping and weeping and weeping. I can't keep the tears from falling from my eyes. I look around. A few people are likewise rapt and weeping, but most people pay no attention to her. I feel rapture and gratitude and fulfillment. After a long while the singing stops and the singer is gone...."

This dream illustrates a symbolic initiation into the path of love. The dreamer is in a place of transition, an airport. He is traveling and waiting for the plane that will take him home, i.e. his spiritual destination. He checks his bags, relinquishing his earthly baggage, and waits to take flight, to lift or be lifted. He is the "man in waiting," sitting in a food court, in hunger, in longing, in the place of nourishment. The food court is a contained space, the courtyard of the Divine. The tables are assembled in a rectangular configuration, around an empty space — the field of actualization, a symbol of wholeness. Empty space is the place of growth and development. He sees a shadowy figure, unrealized, which he interprets as himself, a poet. And he is enraptured by the image of the Lady — "tall, slender, pale, Gaelic, with long strawberry blonde hair" — the Beloved, whose song penetrates the deepest layers of his soul, stripping away the dead leaves of earthly experience. He weeps, the salt of his tears cleansing and purifying his soul. He sees her and his encounter is one of gratitude and fulfillment. She disappears, and the Lover in pursuit of the Beloved is awakened.

The Art of Courtship

The etymology of "courtship" stems from "court" which in Latin and Old French signifies an enclosed yard and/or those assembled in the yard. "Courtship" is defined as "to seek to gain or achieve, to seek the affections of, especially to seek to win a pledge of marriage, to seek to attract...." The key here is that courtship signifies spontaneous actions which became to some degree codified and ritualized, and which took place in the confines of the court, in the enclosed lives of the high-born, wealthy, educated, and noble. The refinement of sentiment and manners that took place engendered the words "courteous," "courtesy," "curtsy," and "courtesan" (a woman of the court).

Courtship is the realm of the sacred erotic, a type of Eros found in the human longing for the Divine, the Holy Other in him/her. Courtly love manifested at a time when marriage was based on economic and political contracts arranged by families. A woman was property to be bought and sold;

she had no rights, but she had value. It was the duty and obligation of the couple to uphold these commitments. There was no room for passion or romance; these feelings were considered instinctual and unrefined, making one impure and carnal. Romantic love activates passion and devotion between lovers. The freedom of the imagination in relation to the divine is integral to courtly love. The soul is uplifted from the mundane to the heavens, and the bond that develops between the lovers is like no other territory of the heart.

The chaos of love is a symptom of the culture at this time; it is due to the loss of love as a spiritual experience. We are plagued by an epidemic of android existence and emotional distance. Eros is wrought with distorted interpretations and acts of perversion. We are disassociated from our senses and the field of the sensual. Gender wars between the sexes split us from our androgynous nature. Capitalistic stress starves us into obesity and reduces the body to a machine. Sky high divorce rates tear families apart. Intimacy issues erode our ability to relate, to connect and express empathy. This is the result of violence and trauma to the heart. The collective symptom is the abandonment of love. Chaos is the call to realize love. The path of love awaits as a divine invitation. We are being invited to realize that each and every one of us is a mystery unfolding, as we attend to the revelations catalyzed by a "true love" experience.

The great desire for the Beloved, while always present, emerges from background to foreground. Throughout the ages wisdom has been guarded by the mystics and flourishes when the consciousness of humanity is ready and fertile to receive the teachings. Eternal wisdom flows from a single source from which all existence emanates; it draws the individual soul toward mystical union. The mystical traditions emphasize a dramatic inward journey of anguish, grief, loss, redemption, joy, and ecstasy of union. The emerging archetypal figure in courtship is the Beloved. There is eternal wisdom, stemming from direct communion with the ultimate reality present in all these great works on the mysteries of love.

The art of courtship is the invocation and evocation of the formless into form; it is an organic process, galvanized by the desire to seek and gain love and affection. Courtship is a sacred practice. The man and the lady agree to engage in a relationship, a dialogue of song and poesis, descending from the mystical realm of divine love. They are each other's reflection of the Imago Dei, Image of God/Goddess, the divine ideal, as each is the other's love, lover, and beloved. Their courtship is the practice of divine remembrance. It is the communication and the spiritual realization of the presence of the divine in the other. Courtship is an eternal engagement. The regal container of "the court" holds the elegant dance between psyche and Eros. The court is a crucible in the midst of the fires of love, galvanizing union between lover and beloved, preparing the bride and bridegroom to enter the domain of the mystical marriage, the *hieros gamos*.

The most likely source for the conventions of courtly love is the Sufi love poetry of Andalusia. Throughout the Islamic world of the ninth and tenth centuries the ideas of love for love's sake and the exaltation of the beloved were prevalent, expressed in the *Risala fi'l-Ishq* (Treatise on Love) of Ibn Sina (Avicenna) in early eleventh century Persia, and culminating in the love poetry of Ibn Arabi, Rumi, and Hafiz. Islamic influences also came back from the Holy Land with the Crusaders. Many other cultural streams can be seen in troubadour poetry, but the initial impulse came from Andalusia.

The troubadour tradition arose in the eleventh century in Occitania (Provence), but over subsequent centuries it spread into Italy, Spain, northern France, England, and Germany. What began as imaginative literature eventually became a philosophy of courtly love that was prevalent in the courts of Europe during its peak in the thirteenth century, before finally dying out in the fourteenth century. The "Mystical Queen" in time went underground, as the Church reasserted its influence in Southern France, proclaiming the troubadours and *trobairitz*, "agents of the Devil." This signaled the waning of the culture of courtly love.

In contemporary society "Christian courtship" is offered as an alternative to "secular dating." The modern Christian paradigm, heavy with Biblical and parental controls, is the antithesis of medieval courtly love, which took place outside the conventions of marriage and aimed at the ennoblement and salvation of the individual soul apart from the authority of the church. Modern Christian "courtship" translates love out of union with the divine into union with an institution. The marriage ideal has been manipulated and dictated by societal norms, diluting the sacred to the literal, resulting in a kind of divine nostalgia, the call for a return to the sacred. It is imperative to revisit and reclaim a wisdom that harmonizes and unites us in love, rather than divorces us from love. Our goal is to explore a more modern dimension of courtship as a spiritually oriented love, having roots in the medieval, rather than the Christian, paradigm.

Modern courtship is experienced by dating, going to movies, sharing a meal, by hanging out and hooking up. Courtship has come out of the court and into the parlor, from the parlor to the porch, from the front porch to the back seat, from the car to the bar, and from the bar to cyberspace. Courtship is abruptly short-circuited by continual disconnects and rising symptoms in the culture. Developing relational stages of intimacy over time are replaced by virtual dating in cyberspace. Conversations are done through e-mail and text messaging. No time is needed to learn about your date. You can google for bios and visit Facebook. Online gifts and e-cards are sent to woo. Techno-courting is the movement taking hold in our new century, and the trend is a framework that has no body.

Contrary to these movements, there is a counterpoint. Among many there are hearts and voices seeking to deinstitutionalize love, who truly desire a world of deep meaning and soulful relating. Courtly love exists in a spiritual dimension, and it can only be experienced in this way. Eros needs a body. Eros has an intention to produce a synergy between lover and beloved. The erotic dimension is the catalyst for the union of spirit and matter. The spirit of the sacred is inherent in breath, animating itself in flesh and form.

Our goal is to return to courtship as a spiritual path. Courtship assists us in unearthing and remembering that just as "I am" so also "You are." We do this by reacquainting ourselves with the knowledge of divine wisdom.

Courtship is a model of relatedness vs. nonrelational interaction. The art of courtship is dialogic vs. monologic. Courtship involves an interchange of energies between two people as a felt experience in the body. In a courtship there is a co-creative intermingling of the feminine and masculine which promotes androgynous consciousness. It is the equality of love between the sexes. Courtship is a conversation which involves communion. And among many other attributes, the art of courtship is the path of love that ultimately takes us on the journey which returns us home. Welcome to love.

Chapter Two
Personal Mythology

As the aspirant progresses on the path, he/she is confronted by many beliefs, ideas, and identities which limit the ability to experience love. In order to progress and deepen, one must rectify false beliefs and limiting behaviors. One's ego undergoes a confrontation with the dark shadows of the unconscious. Mistaken beliefs and false identities blaze in the fires of purification, dissolving the pre-existing myths that veil oneself from the Beloved. Navigating the territory is a dangerous undertaking of tests, trials, and tribulations.

When we open our hearts to love, we open ourselves to joy and to pain, to bliss and to agony. The pain and suffering we experience arise from the expansiveness of love coming up against the limitations of our humanity, love coming up against fear and shame, against sorrow and rage, against self-limiting behaviors and feelings we all have, although the specific form of these limitations is unique to each individual.

We begin with the intimate encounter of falling in love with another person. That is the gift we are given. But soon thereafter we begin to encounter obstacles. We may encounter external obstacles. But even if the world does not interfere with our union, we likely will encounter the internal obstacles of our emotional complexities which are constructed in reaction to the cultural, familial, and personal mythologies we are caught in. Along with hearts and flowers, trysts and escapades, the path to true love begins with self-examination and personal work on our own selves.

Cultural Myths

Cultural myths profess the fundamental world view of a people. They explain the creation stories, spiritual customs, and ideals of a society. Eventually they come to be a cultural narrative. The powerful domination of the cultural narrative affects individuals, families, and societies. Cultural myths dictate rules and moral codes as if they are the only possible ones to take, even if those positions are not useful to the individual or family as a whole. Culture is designed to perpetuate viewpoints, processes, and stories that serve those who benefit from that culture but may work against the freedom and functionality of the individual. Identifying the impact of the establishment on the individual allows greater freedom from the oppression of external constructs.

It is expected by society that everyone will grow up and make a positive contribution. Often you will hear, "Someday you will grow up and get married." But some people are not marriage material. They thrive on personal freedom and creativity. They want to use their procreative energies for service in the world. They are more inclined towards poetry, art, the spiritual, and seek family in those arenas, in intentional communities which support like-minded individuals. And yet they can't bear the pressure and expectations made by their culture and family to marry and reproduce. They surrender their freedom and encounter ongoing depression and feelings of repression. They live their lives as imposters and reproduce dysfunctional outcomes that are the result of their lack of personal integrity. Many people live under the pressure of the "tyranny of shoulds" — "I should do this," "I should have done that" — that give rise to an externalized self, a self which appears to be safer and more loveable. Contrary to the cultural "ideal person," there is a "real self" that is vital and unique. Inner conflict and neurosis results when an individual turns away from the "real self," which has potential for healthy growth, to an idealized self dictated by the socially appropriate.

Personal Myths

Each of us is born into a story. Individuals define who they are based on the stories adults reflect and tell them about themselves when they are children. When we tell our stories, we recite events which can be either true or fictitious. The personal narrative reveals the structure of one's psyche, the limitations and defenses of a person's ego.

The personal story has a deep influence on life scripts, which constellate into a personal mythology. Each story is true for the person telling it. Individuals construct the meaning of life in interpretive stories which are treated as "the truth." The construction of meaning can be monological (by oneself) or dialogical (with others) — with the latter having the greater power in our lives because we are social beings. In this sense, an individual is a socially constructed narrative system.

Our personal myth is the story we tell about ourselves, who we are, our purpose and our life destiny. A fictitious myth is often the story you have been told by external authorities that debilitates the real self. Our personal myths become deeply ingrained as the inner psychological story. These myths influence and shape our personality. Content produced by the imagination is not necessarily based on fact. Mistaken beliefs are faulty, self-defeating perceptions and attitudes, a type of fiction that is an imaginative creation that does not represent actuality. These stories have an everlasting effect on self-identity and the journey one will take or will not take.

Complexes and Contracts

How does our personal myth influence our life story? How does the psychological impact of unconscious and unresolved life material translate as "the same old story"? Freud tells us unconscious forces may interfere with conscious intentions. This conflict produces irrational thoughts and behaviors. The unconscious generates conflicts, repetitive behaviors, and destructive patterns which recycle and have negative influences on a person's life. This experience is incongruent with desired goals and forms an intra-psychic net of complexities. Personal myths and stories are bound by these complexities, resulting in the unconscious reenactment of one's personal story throughout one's life.

"You're a very complex person!" "You are so complicated!" "I just can't deal with you!" Does this all sound familiar? Before you even get to know a person, you can experience all kinds of complications. Just getting together for a cup of tea turns out to be a protracted negotiation. And how about the people who think they know you before they do and try to tell you who you are?

Complexes have their origins in personal and collective wounds that have not been dealt with. Out of the wound various ways of relating and behaving form that repeatedly recreate themselves and are driven by our personal narrative, our inner identity, which may cause inconsistent relating and attract dysfunction. These are all unconscious behaviors we learned and repressed as children, mostly for the sake of survival. As adults we lack the skills to effectively deal with things in a different way. The learned strategy for coping is to ignore, excuse, and blame the other person for "the problem"; to defend, disassociate, and self-medicate in order to survive the pain. Repeating the same strategies of repression that began in early childhood leads to the accumulation of a dark shadow. Ego strength and psychological resilience leave some people less affected than others. Nonetheless, our lives can become a tragic comedy in which we take on the main character in the movie *Groundhog Day*, wherein the same drama plays itself over and over again. It's as if we are a magnet that draws the dynamic into our life.

The "same old story" is a repetitive drama that indicates severe wounding or early childhood trauma that has remained unconscious. Complexities cluster around the wound, drawing familiar experiences that reinforce and give the repressed material autonomous psychic life in relationships. Unexamined and unconscious, the wounding snowballs into extravagant and psychologically devastating outcomes.

Salt in the Wound: You Lick Mine, I'll Lick Yours

Unresolved wounds attract others with similar wounding. For example, two people who come from abusive backgrounds find each other. Their attraction is an unconscious agreement to take care of each other's wound — "I'll lick yours, if you'll lick mine" — forming bonds and giving both the experience of healing through love. It's as if these two people and no other can understand each other's worlds. They share feelings of repulsion towards humanity on the same exact themes. It is familiar and familial. In the initial stage of a relationship this can be felt as incredibly liberating. But what initially attracts can eventually repulse. Repulsion tends to set in when the wound collapses inward and inflicts the couple, infecting them with paralyzing effects and recreating the original trauma. Unable to grow beyond the complex, they find themselves rewounding each other.

Inter-generational Complex: The Family Secret

There are scenarios which are the shadow business of a family secret. We could refer to this as the "inherent complex." As an example, two young lovers who find themselves attracted to each other eventually learn that neither of them knew their fathers. In both families the father's identity was kept a secret, affecting them both in their sense of wholeness and esteem. With each other they ward off the shame and feelings of alienation in their socio-cultural environment. The bonding deepens due to the wound. He loves that she can understand his emotional world. She loves that he accepts her as she is.

As with most young loves, in time they part ways. She discovers the identity of her father. He was told the name of a man who was not his father. This young man always suffered from a certain dark "feeling" that he could not identify. He became addicted to heroin; it was the only thing that would take that "feeling" away. All of his life he searched to find an answer to this "feeling." Eventually he died from a heroin overdose. After his death, his family admitted who his father was, and oddly enough his father, now dead, was a heroin addict. That "feeling" was the lifelong symptom of heroin in the blood. The psyche, kept in the shadows, abducted by the family secret, lives out the answer to that which it seeks.

Love Projects

What is that terrible feeling? You're going along with your life, feeling spirited, uplifted, feeling good about yourself, and then you meet them. They're a little different. They don't hold your interest for very long, but you hold theirs. Their attraction is flattering and their attention endearing to you. Maybe they're not what you're looking for, but they have been looking for you. You feel a little empathic. They're odd and really need someone to care for them. Maybe you can help them out. You get hooked by their potential, their brilliance, and their inner beauty — by the light only you can see. They need somebody to love them — and you volunteer. Before you know it you have a "love project" on your hands, a project that seems to occupy your time and energy, not leaving much for anyone or anything else.

When you're with them it's as if you cross a threshold and enter another world, their wounded world. As time goes on they demand more from you. You are not doing it right or quite fulfilling their needs, and, by the way, you are to have no needs. You can be in the best of moods, but when you see them, within seconds flat they bring you down. It's like a blow to the belly. You lose your joy and feel a pang in the heart. Something drops out and you deflate. They are killjoys, "soul muggers," who produce the feeling of soul loss. Dimensions of yourself are smothered and desecrated by sarcasm: "yeah but," "that's not so great," and the ubiquitous "whatever." It is as if you are the hot air balloon, and your supposed lover is nothing more than a sandbag that brings you down. You stoke the fire, which lifts, and they drag you down. They are not interested in your best interest. With deep sighs and labored breaths, they can barely say, "I am happy for you." They would rather talk about how unhappy they are and how unhappy you make them. Your family, your friends, even your pets can't stand to be around them. And you have faith and hope that your love will transform them and the light you see will beholden to all....

Faith is being sure of what we hope for and certain of what we do not see. Hope is a form of denial, denying what is occurring in order to postulate what you want to have occur. You can lose yourself to hope and faith. You forget what is happening to you because you only see what the other needs. Hope can be a deadening force that perpetuates self harm. It is wrought with "if onlys." "If there is something wrong, it must be me." "What can I do to make it better?" "I hope I can change this, I hope they will get it." "If only I could...." Hope reinforces unhealthy situations, which can become a life of entrapment and soul loss.

Love projects stick to your shoe like a wad of gum, like taffy: you get caught in it and it gets all over you, leaving you with a big mess. Love projects are problems that get worse the more you struggle against them. They are mean. They bully. They thrive on put-down teasing. They are people who have no control over themselves, so they gain a sense of power by controlling you. Your spiritual connection is denied. They do not validate. They withdraw and abandon for no apparent reason. They are secretive and have a secret life. They are keen on self-neglect. They draw from you in the name of love, and you feel drained. You think it's love, and aimlessly exist in a trance state. You find yourself out of balance, disoriented, with no sense of self, losing your confidence, and doubting your perceptions. These are symptoms of soul loss and self-depredation. Love projects use their intelligence as a weapon to blame, manipulate, and confuse. Lost in the merge, you internalize their shame and humiliation. Their moods are volatile and intimidating. Their answers are short and aggressive. Any question is an automatic invitation to war. They need you, they love you, and they won't let you go, while simultaneously you repulse and disgust them. And before you know it you have become one of their haunting ghosts.

Unconscious Contracts

The unconscious contract of the culture is the agreement to follow the rules and regulations of external authorities, religious, parental, and familial. To contract means to agree and also to shrink, as in contraction. An unconscious family contract is developed out of agreements that have strong boundaries — for example, the agreement not to discuss emotional issues, to be polite, to keep secrets. Family contracts can come into conflict when two people from different backgrounds and cultures come together. One family background is emotionally expressive, sometimes causing intense disharmony and drama, while the partner is from an emotionally repressive family whose contract is to withdraw from discussing or working through emotional situations. These silent, yet powerful, ways of relating stream into and become their own new relationship contracts. Unconsciously each partner adheres to certain ways of being and relating with the other. Because it is unconscious, it leaves the soul vulnerable to suffering loss.

It is not unusual for one of the partners in this kind of relationship to take actions which make conscious the behaviors causing them to feel unfulfilled. The one partner matures and develops while the other partner remains in the comfort zone. This is a danger zone — watch out! The growth-producing partner is motivated to revise the unconscious contracts and make conscious choices which are satisfying and more meaningful to his or her life. This causes tremendous chaos in a stable and stale relationship. Gems are born from chaos. Out of the chaos and revision, something new can be birthed between the couple. The biggest difficulty is when the comfortable partner denies the dissatisfaction, seeing no need for self-examination or why the other "once happy" mate needs to change a thing, and refuses to budge. This is a common and most unfortunate outcome.

Change is the natural opportunity for engaging the courtship and evolving the relationship into a deeper level of love and growth. The truth is that everything is always changing, whether we are conscious of it or not, just as in the early stages of the courtship. It doesn't stop because of our contracts. Rather,

23

now that the relationship has a container, it can gain momentum and excel. There are ups, downs, plateaus, and growing pains in every relationship. This is what ignites the passion, the courtship. Courtship exists through time and reveals the purpose the relationship has to fulfill. The death of outdated contracts awakens us to the love, and allows us to gain gratitude for the experience.

Archetypes

Myths are archetypal stories. Archetypes are energies that feel "bigger than big." They have the capacity to initiate, influence, and mediate the behavioral characteristics and typical experiences of all human beings. They transcend race, culture, history, and geography. Archetypes pre-exist in the collective unconscious as predetermined patterns of being and perceiving. These patterns are at the innate center of the human psyche, a part of the collective memory. Archetypes evoke images, feelings, and themes that are universal.

Love is universal. Love has no gender. There are archetypes one may encounter on the journey of love. They, too, have an androgynous nature and are experienced by both men and women on the path of love. Courtship confronts each of us about the work we need to do both in collective memory and collective healing. Developmentally, psychosocially, physically, and spiritually, throughout the various stages of our life, we experience our shadow, our narcissism, our ecstatic lover, our mystic, our dominator personality, our stormy moods, our eroticism and passion, and our Self as Beloved.

Archetypal encounters are typically experienced by people who live their life in search of meaning. They awaken us from our slumber and carry the potential for self revelation and divine illumination. This passage cultivates the maturity of the soul and self reliance gained by personal wisdom.

Archetypal abduction occurs when one is too open and weak, lacking boundaries, and susceptible to psychic influences. Abduction also occurs through victimization and original wounds, those places in one's psyche that may be in arrested development, unconsciously seeking experiences that will complete and heal soul loss. They can even be activated in childhood through imaginary figures that carry a strong archetypal resonance with you and contribute to a fantasy you may have about yourself. Archetypal influences are indicated when you find yourself in situations or behaviors that are out of character, which normally you would not allow yourself to participate in. The key is the activation of the unconscious, a part of your self seeking integration.

People are prone to archetypal influences for many reasons. Trauma, early loss, abandonment, and abuse are some examples of stressors that produce gaps in the psyche. There is a natural inclination to seek what has been lost or is missing from the developmental experience. For some this is conscious seeking, for others it is unconscious. When it comes to the journey of love, there is an attraction to the unknown territories yet to be discovered. At the core of this mystery are those attributes of one's self seeking to be known, often measured against those individuals who have integrated and developed these attributes in themselves.

For example, the "love experience" is a collective memory. If one doesn't know or experience love, one may hear oneself asking the question: "Where is love?" The feeling manifests as a gap in the personality, a lacuna in the psyche, and is experienced as a kind of emotional amnesia. There is no personal memory of the love experience. But because it is a collective experience, intuitively a person who is missing the experience knows it exists. On a very deep and sincere level, the experiencer knows the memory is incomplete.

When the love experience is absent from the scope of one's perception and experience, symptoms of loss and alienation affect one's ability to relate in a healthy way. Undeveloped perceptions taint intimacies and make it difficult to be consistent in relationships. Deep loss and heartfelt desires produce a rich interior life, activating imaginary figures. A child who needs, wants, and desires protection may imagine a guardian angel, a figure imbued with magical powers. A child who has no mother invokes the Divine Mother or Goddess, or a child without a father, a Father God.

The process of recollection is integral to discovering and developing one's psyche towards wholeness and completion. These creative archetypal forms transcend time and space, and emerge from the depth world to complete what is incomplete. The essential and the existential connect. Our essential need draws from what exists, and when it is experienced, it is a mystical encounter producing a shift in consciousness. And with each encounter, we integrate the external as internal. We access our spiritual nature and actualize our true self. The love experience evolves and matures as a felt state of deep connection, growing and integrating as the embodiment of the Divine.

Archetypal Encounters

There are people with certain energies that keep recreating themselves through time as archetypes and prototypes. It is possible that they are just part of the master plan. Their presence here is just as necessary as anyone else's, in the representation of the divine play. They are here to awaken us, heal us, and force us into our own recovery, to teach us to transcend and learn, tolerate and forgive, gain spiritual experience, reduce our pride and taste humility.

The light of love reveals the dark shadows of our woundedness, our unredeemed complexities, our unrealized potential, and the denseness of our humanity. Love casts light on all that we could be and are not, due to our painful limitations, and more often than not casts that shadow on to that "other" person who seems to match our own desire to be more alive. Simply put, the one with repressed libido may be attracted to someone who fully expresses her libido. The one who has not actualized her power may be drawn to a powerful man, and look to him to have the power she knows not yet. We are attracted to what we are but may not have realized yet. When we have not acknowledged our own power, lust, desire, anger, intelligence, sorrow, or ecstasy, we will tend to project those qualities on another person (who may be doing the same thing to us) and trap that person (or our perception of that person) in our shadow. We are attracted to "others" who seem to act out our shadow. The light of love reveals this so that we can reclaim our unloved shadow material and love ourselves and the "other" in the fullness of our potential.

We need to be aware of the ways that personal myths and abduction by archetypal figures, within and without, can limit love, growth, and connection with a deeper story. We need to be conscious of the story of the false self, which perpetuates disharmony and dysfunction, and how it affects the narrative of two people committed to conscious courtship. In order for the archetype of the Beloved to emerge, we have to clear the debris of the heart. There are many traps a lover may encounter. We need to be aware of how our shadow material influences the way we love and experience love. On the path of love, we encounter many relationships stuck in dramas with mythic figures, archetypal figures to whom we are compellingly attracted.

Dionysus is the lover who drives you mad. The Hades lover takes you to hell and back. Zeus is the successful patriarch who does not prove to be a very good lover. And watch out for Poseidon — you are in for stormy weather. Eros as the lover joins with Psyche. The integration and transcendence of all image and duality is the Beloved. Not everyone has all of these encounters, but they do pervade the human experience. For the purpose of this expedition into the shadow of love, archetypal figures are as much male as they are female, and female as much as they are male.

Wild Lovers: Let It Rip

People on the path seeking love in spiritual arenas are likely to encounter Dionysian lovers. Their eternally youthful appearance and androgynous nature stands out in the crowd. They possess mystical qualities and a lack of inhibitions that are a lure for the bored. You find them praying, chanting, drumming, and dancing, and they draw you into their trance. It is an arousing energetic exchange, which unravels your state of steadiness and assuredness. Especially for the uninitiated, this ecstatic lover is very powerful. Their erotic intensity unravels your thread, pulling you out of one solid pattern into a different one. They are deep and inviting and erotically enticing. They are an intense emotional roller coaster ride, taking you to the high of highs and the low of lows. Their passion stirs and draws in a love interest, but they can't be mated or committed to any one person. They detest obligation and drive their lovers mad with jealousy. They are wanderers who thrive on intense encounters and move on to avoid a lover's expectations. These *puers* and *puellas* are impulsive and undependable, so don't wait too long for them to show up or make that call.

Bad, Bad Boys and Bad, Bad Girls: Hades Lovers

Hades characters have been wounded by the world. Their disposition is antisocial and they prefer to withdraw into their darkness. They tend to be invisible and are comfortable in seclusion. Their paranoid and suspicious nature is in a constant battle with the "real world." They are depressive, oppressive, and unable to recognize that they are prisoners of their own interior dark existence. Hades people don't court: they seduce, stalk, abduct, and inadvertently keep showing up in your life, giving you the impression that you are drawn together by fate. They have a psychic instinct towards your vulnerabilities and captivate you into their secret world. Hades people live out of an imagined fantasy of who you are. When you don't fulfill their imagined point of view, Hades is enraged and invades and breaks you down. Their sexual interest with you is dependent on your ability to converse with their wounded world. They are desperate for a soul connection. The ability to connect to their deep inner world is rewarded by ecstatic sex that can be exciting yet frustrating. They get into intense physical coupling, but the warmth and generosity of love tends to be absent. They take their satisfaction but leave their partner unsatisfied. They slake their lust but cannot feel the love. The Hades relationship goes nowhere and is nothing more than a deep dark hole. And you wonder: "What is a great person like me doing with someone like this?"

The Queen of the Underworld

"One day I told a friend about my encounter with a Hades man. I told her I never needed to have this dark experience; it was painful, even awful. She listened carefully and said, 'Yes, it is a painful journey to undergo descent into the underworld, and now you are no longer naïve. You know the territory.' She went on,

'Having traveled through to the other side, rather than being the subject, you are now the Queen.'"

Kings and Queens: Power Lovers

Patriarchal lovers are endemic in the culture and common on the path of love. They are the type of people who look good, smell good in their expensive colognes and perfumes, and stand high on the mountain casting their bolts of power into the field. They are dominant, successful, intelligent, convincing, and no one's equal. They are selfish and make no excuse for it. Distancing from any emotional entanglements, they are blatantly arrogant. Zeus figures hold all the power in a relationship. They seek out well-trained submissives who are emotionally empty and who live their lives through others, prone to dominant, authoritative types. People who lack their own power and authority placate and pacify this God/dess. Have you ever been as turned on as you are by a powerful authority figure? The heat is so steamy that great sex is a guarantee — until you get in bed and wonder what the hell happened. These power lovers are great seducers who lack passion. They are lousy lovers and sexually dominate to get their needs met. These kings and queens get married, stay married, and have multiple affairs and dalliances to keep their power in the field.

Stormy Types: In the Sea of Love

Stormy lovers live down in the deep. Their emotions and instincts easily drown out the feelings of others. They are psychically powerful, intense, and penetrating, and you find yourself tumbling over yourself to fulfill their desires. They exert tremendous unconscious influence, as they live and reside out of intense depth, giving them power, dominance, and control over your innermost secrets. At the mercy of their own waves, they are exhausting and disempowering types to love. Sex is driven purely by instinct, making them horrible lovers who lack sensitivity or concern for the partner's needs. You are easily washed away if you rely on them for any emotional or physical comfort. Your demands are breaks in their waves crashing and dispersing them into an endless supply of sea foam. While there may be plenty of fish in the sea, you had better watch out for this whopper.

Wounded Birds

These gentle, wounded souls are drawn by your empathy into your sympathy and feed on the attention you give to their emotional pain. They sing their sad stories night and day. You are flattered by their attention, by the respect and gratitude they give you, because it soothes your own woundedness to offer counsel to someone more wounded than yourself. But after a while it seems like it is all give and no take, like you are a receptacle for the litany of their unending complaints. It is all monologue, no dialogue. They don't really want healing; they just want to keep on squealing. What need of yours is being met by letting these wounded birds peck at your breast?

Narcissus and Echo, Echo, Anybody Home? Can You Hear Me?

Narcissists are amazingly beautiful. Their beauty is a lure. They can see no other, love no other, reject all those who are drawn to them, and leave behind a trail of broken hearts. They cannot and do not fall in love with anyone else. Narcissists can only fall in love with their own image. They are people who don't reflect you or your voice. Your existence is invisible to them. You are no more than an echo. Be aware of the signs and the symptoms you feel when you love a Narcissus type. You are invisible, neither seen nor heard. It is disconcerting to have your own self-image shattered in order to maintain theirs. You are "trapped in their mirror." Narcissists forever linger, mesmerized by their own brilliance, their intelligence, their wants and needs, their grandiose dreams, drifting in the endless monologue of their own story.

Dark Eros

Metabolizing unprocessed emotional material for our partners is neither unusual nor easy. As the courtship progresses, unfinished business and personal issues present themselves. This can be a very difficult time for the couple. You may discover that you are not seen in your own true light, rather in the shadow of a light that is projected on you. You are entangled with someone who doesn't know himself and depends on you to figure him out. Your "real" is unbearable to your partner. If you are not strong in your identity and self-esteem, you could lose your self.

"With B., I never knew who he was relating to. He would talk to me as if I were some other person, not me, and become enraged when I spoke and honored myself. He saw someone else, his haunting ghosts and fantasy images, and when I did not meet his fantasy images, his ghosts would haunt me."

Sometimes you have to break away and let your lover slay his own dragons and deal with her own haunting ghosts. It is not your work to master someone else's dragons. The work of the dragon master is to collapse and reclaim the projections, and take responsibility for addressing one's own psyche and fulfilling one's own needs. Then one can be emotionally available to grow in a consistent and healthy love experience with you.

Passionate love has been characterized as dramatic, obsessive, and potentially violent — although passion itself is not violent. It is the danger of depending on your love object to validate your own inner desires that can result in frustration and outrage. The lover projects her fantasy image onto a "person." The lover relates to their "other" as if he is "another." In time this erodes any type of interpersonal connection. For example, it is a very powerful experience to find a lover who knows how to have fulfilling sex with you and you with him. It feels like God has given you everything you ever wanted. Tremendous emphasis is placed on the sexual experience, which short circuits the courtship. You both decide you have found who you are looking for. Very little time is given to knowing each other. All you want to know is that you are each other's ideal sex mate. This is a dangerous assumption, which can lead to a backwards type of courtship.

This approach is out of balance, and more often than not leads to intense dysfunction. Interactions outside the bedroom are thwarted. The lovers learn they are actually very different. She expresses her opinions and ideas. He argues with her, insisting she respond in certain ways. She has no idea to whom or what he is relating. He is relating to a fantasy, not to her true and unique self. These interactions result in anger, even rage. Although she has compassion for his needs, she has no idea how to fulfill them without partic- ipating in pretension. She is his ideal sexual fantasy in the bedroom, but when she becomes a person with her own independent sense of self, his perceptions of her are delusional. He is dependent on and vulnerable to her to fulfill his ideal. Eventually he becomes more insistent, controlling, and abusive. When she is weak, she is susceptible to his criticism and beliefs, his shaping and molding. She suffers soul loss, becoming a prisoner to his image.

Consider this: love between two people can be experienced differently by each person. The lover's stored-up depth and potency finds solace in the presence of the beloved, but this gives rise to aggression when he deflects her ideal. She is indebted to him out of her need to express "her love," not necessarily "the love" that they have been given. Without a strong foundation of trust and rapport between them, they are essentially strangers playing out characters in a twisted drama. It is the charge disconnected from the battery. Every spiritual path, including the path of love, recognizes source as essential.

Deceptive Perceptions

Be aware of delusions and deceptive perceptions. The tendency to be quick to assign meaning to an encounter comes out of our own eagerness to find our mate. One may assign too much authority to a new acquaintance with whom one has a connection. Connections influence initial perceptions — but they do not rule out your tendency to deceive yourself. For example, you meet someone who automatically thinks he knows who you are, and acts as if she can and does intuit your needs. When a person is aligned with you and your needs, it is enticing and exciting. The soul longs for deep connection, and these people are seeking out your longing.

Longing is the common denominator which translates the experience into a direct connection with each other's soul and spirit. This yearning locates us in a very delicate territory. The soul is universal. So when two people connect it is quick to be interpreted as meaningful — as it is. It is impossible not to be connected. Ultimately we are all connected in spirit. We are all spiritual beings in human forms with personalities, histories, and complexities.

But take your time assigning specific meaning to every connection. Take your time with the courtship, and ask yourself some questions about the connection. Is the connection peaceful, harmonious, and consistent over the course of time? As time goes on, do you find yourself soul mugging (a tendency to stay hidden) rather than soul making (expressing and co-creating)? Are you enthusiastic about genuinely knowing the other person, or are you more interested in figuring out what it is they think and feel about you? Do you feel present, or are you filtering through interpretations and seeking evidence to remain in the encounter? Ask yourself, "What's the hurry?"

We are always experiencing divine encounters, with or without another person. The "Other" is always present. Entertain the idea that it is more usual than unusual to experience connection and universality. Courtship informs us beyond the obvious. We are inspired to come together not only to be with what is known but also to be with that which is unknown. Truly being present with another allows the unknown to reveal itself through the manifestation of two beings. The purpose, then, of courtship is to establish an intimate relationship to the unknown seeking to be known, which may disclose to us genuine, authentic love.

Romance and Stability

Romance has its shadow, a "dark Eros." Erotic realms of the unknown produce fear. Fear is assuaged by reason and stability. Reason and stability equally have a shadow realm. Eros is instinctual and aggressive. Stability is habitual and boring. Dark Eros is chaotic, with no love and no connection. Any time you try to establish trust or intimacy, it collapses.

If you fall into Eros without establishing a bond and a general idea of the person you are with, then you are vulnerable to dark passion, suffering, and drama. It feels romantic, but it is driven by aggression, control, and instinct. You think you're in love with them because you're entwined with their energy and having phenomenal sex. Lovers expressing dark Eros are merely figments of each other's imagination. "She is a beast in and out of the sack."

Romantic passion is a natural outflow of mutual love, respect, and consideration. It sounds like: "He is such a good man and a real erotic animal" — a natural rather than an adrenal state. One does not experience extremes, but states of balance that are reinforced by love and nurturance. There is an interchange between stability and depth. What connects us to romantic passion begins with our own personal courtship of love.

Relationships amplify what is lacking in the other. A person who grows up in a dysfunctional environment and is invited into a functional situation has a really hard time. He is in a foreign land, lacking the resources and skills to relate in that territory. These are delicate situations when one or the other partner may have a knight-like quality of rescue or a goddess-like quality of transformation. Often, her/his shadow is liberating to the other. She dares to live out of places she's been restricted from and so does he. This is extremely inviting, attractive, and magnetic — the highly repressed individual seeking the highly expressed individual.

Dispelling the Myth: Early Childhood Loss

The stories we tell ourselves about ourselves leave us vulnerable to these many types of archetypal encounters. We define who we are based on the stories adults reflect and tell us about ourselves when we are children. One of the most influential is the birth story. I believe the birth story has a lasting impression on the soul. One's own personal story has had a deep influence on one's life script. Throughout psychological development thoughts, feelings, and memories group themselves into dynamic clusters which function like sub-personalities. Unresolved and repressed issues accumulate around the central core of the personality.

Unraveling the story can be a lifelong journey, involving questioning one's mysterious existence and pondering one's own mythology. "Who am I?" "What is my purpose?" "What is my destiny?" These questions erupt at different stages of life. And with every inquiry there is a new discovery. Every time the complex is triggered one can feel tortured, even cursed, by one's history. Personal wounds produce a deep and relentless sorrow. Characteristics of these complexities are a sense of unworthiness, rejection, shame, anger, rage, and despair.

There is usually an external encounter (a new relationship, family dynamics, difficulties at the workplace) which activates the triggers. Through self-inquiry, unconscious material surfaces, seeking one's attention. Often these triggers orginate in one's family of origin; they collectively constellate as a universal shadow. Blood shadows, family secrets, bad blood between people, and family feuds — these can be so painful that people have described them as a "family curse."

The constancy of a trusted analysis attends to the "curse" and the truth reveals itself in the dialogue of personal suffering. Recognition and exploration of the wound are the precursors to Self-realization. The process of confrontation with the shadow, the purification and refinement of the personality, catalyzes a transition from a state of victimization to one of self-acceptance. Hence, it is important to approach triggers with compassion rather than disgust. "You can't change early life experiences but you can change your interpretation of them."

Early loss is even trickier. The problem with early loss is that you don't have a full range of what you're looking at, since a young person isn't capable of seeing the bigger picture. Early childhood loss is experienced as abandonment. At age two a child cannot differentiate. At this age one is the center of the universe. The individual feels rejected and the tendency is to overpersonalize and internalize the losses.

Children believe the myths reflected by the adults in their lives. These story lines surface when intimacy is near. "You deserve to be abandoned." "Something is wrong with you." "You are bad and unlovable." This has so much influence on a child because in the early developmental years you are forming your identity. The younger you are when losses occur, the more severe the trauma, so in the future when something triggers loss it revives the identity, i.e., "You deserve to be abandoned." As a child most of who you are develops from what is being reflected by the adults in your life. Adults mirror to the child reflections that are often loaded with distortions. These projections set up a distant sense of self. As a child, the ability to discriminate truth from distortions is difficult because of the dependency on parents, siblings, and community for acceptance and self-worth.

"How do you know who you are? As an adult you have the ability to self-reflect, to stand outside the mirroring of others. You come into your own sense of self, which is achieved through opposition, or breaking away from the external mirroring and entering into internal reflections."

Changing the interpretation begins by recognizing that you had to have an attachment in the first place in order to experience loss. We can be trapped by our feeling states. Ask yourself, "Is this true? Did they leave because they rejected me?" You may discover in some instances the choice to leave was an act of love or had nothing to do with you. When loss is triggered, try to examine the situation, put it under the microscope, and remain objective. Ask yourself if the rejection says something about you — or does it say something about the person who abandons? Ask yourself if you deserve to be rejected. If so, it may be because of your behavior. There is a difference between behavior and being. Behavior is something you can change. Being doesn't change. Being deserves to be respected and has worth.

The death of a relationship is followed by an initial period of shock. We begin to review the relationship, weaving and unweaving stories about the separation, about who did what to whom, who's to blame, who won and who lost. Our moods can fluctuate mercilessly. There is a tendency to obsess and rehearse the humiliations, the injustices, the awful things that were said and done. We settle on a coherent narrative that we can work with internally, analyze, and eventually discard. It takes time to emotionally metabolize our life experiences and move on.

People fester with the belief that if they were good enough, people wouldn't leave. The internal belief is, "If I were good enough, I could go through life and not experience loss." This is simply not true. All human beings experience loss. As an adult you do not need to rehearse how much loss you have had in life. Rehearsing the child's interpretation pulls you into a void, into your own damaged sense of self. As an adult you can examine these beliefs against what you know about human nature. Then the healing can begin.

Rewriting your Personal Story

The fall from love, archetypal encounters reflecting shades of darkness, and living out the "same old story" — all are indicators for change. These experiences ask for a redefinition of self in tandem with a reinterpretation of love. It asks us to change everything: our belief systems, our limiting thoughts and ideas, and the way we mentally process emotions and interact with the environment. To change your story is to change your life. It means letting go of what is familiar. It may mean changing your associations and consciously surrounding yourself with love and support, seeking positive and affirmative people who have an intention to fulfill their life's purpose, choosing to be in the company of healthy role models that spark a light in you, actively surrendering the voices that deny and keep you invisible, and inviting the voices that say, "You go!" "You can do it!" "You are beautiful." "You are loved." The soul's natural state is happiness. Make an appointment to be with yourself. Listen to your inner teacher, the voice who loves and coaches the unseen essence of who you truly are into being.

Seeing is freeing! Dispelling your life myth is to heal the fiction and rework it with your own interpretation. As an adult you have the opportunity to discover the true story through your own inquiry and self-exploration. You possess the wherewithal to rewrite the myth.

Personality can be thought of as the story of a person's life. As the personality changes, we in effect rewrite our life stories, perhaps by changing the future or by the telling of our past from a different point of view. The goal is to loosen the grip of the myth, identify the fiction, and repair mistaken beliefs. In a clear interpretation, an individual's thoughts, feelings, beliefs, convictions, attitudes, and actions become expressions of his or her uniqueness.

The Quest for the Beloved: Psyche and Eros

Psyche, too beautiful for any mortal man to marry, is carried by the wind to a magnificent mountain palace where her every need is fulfilled by invisible servants, until nightfall when her immortal lover, Eros, the god of love, comes to make love with her and sleep with her. His sole condition for coming is that she not light a lamp. He wants to remain invisible to her. When she finally lights a lamp and gazes on his beauty, he vanishes, never to return.

You are alone in the dark, longing for your love. Eros visits and hears your silent secrets, exactly what you need, connecting with you in the pattern of your reality. It is a mystical encounter. He whispers in your ear, reciting paragraphs from your diary, fulfilling your deepest desires and fantasies. He is a living, psychic reality awaiting your vivification. There is excitement and stimulation beyond belief. His presence is a prayer answered.

Eros awakens Psyche to the Beloved. Falling into this love, she is transported into magical realms she never knew existed. Love in the dark, an eternal bond, provokes her erotic potential, her power, the fullness of her being, the unfoldment of her purpose. She descends into the realm of the collective, the spiritual, and encounters the numinous. This is her initiation into the embodiment of love, into the personification of passion. She lifts her light to the dark and sees God — and in a flicker, this presence disappears. Herein begins the quest for the Beloved, a journey that draws her forth to her divine realization.

Bereft, Psyche wanders through the world, looking for her lost love and performing a series of impossible tasks to appease Aphrodite, the goddess of love, the mother of Eros, tasks that are only fulfilled with the aid of other creatures. In the end, Eros goes to the father god Zeus and asks him to give Psyche immortality so that they can be married.

For the love of Eros and union with God, Psyche is subjected to tests and feats beyond her comprehension. She confronts her past fears and sorrows. Taken to task with each test she passes, she expands beyond her mortal limitations. Eros is the vital force that motivates the soul to develop. To pass her rites, she must shuttle between worlds, the personal into the transpersonal and the transpersonal into the personal. Love is the doorway between two worlds, the place where heaven and earth meet. She gathers assistance to her by the whirls of the other. By the accomplishment of her feats, her final descent is ascension to become an immortal Goddess. She enters into divine union with Eros, and they give birth to Bliss.

The work we do advances the work of the world and the collective, evolving consciousness to take us forward. When the archetypal energies are brought into balance, we develop as strong and healthy people and ensoulment occurs. As highly integrated androgynous souls, we enter into an image which itself is transcended.

Chapter Three
Soul Mates: A Myth That Splits

The relinquishment of the false persona is expedited by devotion and perseverance. One becomes completely in love with Love. And thus, as one burns through and to the essence of love, one's longing is ever more ignited. It is important to proceed with caution. Pilgrims not only confront personal mythologies but also have to break through popular cultural beliefs which reinforce dependency on mates who are sanctioned to complete the incomplete. No doubt love relationships can serve as a catalyst to personal awareness. Ultimately the work of realization is an internal exploration which reveals our androgyny, an individual whole and complete unto One-self.

We live in a split consciousness which overlays the psyche of humanity. Splits are inherited rather than inherent. Splits are not essential to our being. One indication of a myth that splits is the ever-pervading mating attitude, the myth of finding one's "soul mate." The term implies reuniting with one's "other half." Finding one's soul mate is identified with the feeling of being with someone whom one has a deep and natural affinity for, which includes love, intimacy, sexual love, and spiritual compatibility. To understand this concept further, it is important to look at how one comes to the belief that a soul mate exists.

One of the most popular philosophies regarding this concept is written in Plato's *Symposium*. At one time, the story goes, we all were androgynous souls consisting equally of male and female gender, called hermaphrodites. Each androgynous being was a rounded whole, forming a complete circle. As a result of hubris toward the gods, our hermaphrodite souls were split into separate genders. Zeus, the Olympian god, divides the human race in two with a bolt of lightning. Each half *yearns* for the half from which it had been severed. This ancient myth, present in modern love today, articulates and professes to explain the innate love which human beings feel for one another, the love which longs to restore us to our ancient state by merging two beings into one and healing the division humanity suffers. The search to find the other half is motivated by the notion that when the two unite they return to wholeness, completion, and totality.

Plato's account serves as an interesting metaphor. Insolence toward the gods splits and separates. The story teaches that a dominant ego-orientation results in confrontation. The ego state ("me") overrides and undermines the sacred "I AM" in relationship to the divine. Severing continues to exist in the collective imagination of humanity. The split, male from female, produces symptoms of despair, depression, alienation, and disassociation. The physical body, once sacred, is incomplete.

This split has been perpetuated by social systems, gender-based psychologies, philosophies, and spiritual systems. Humanity finds itself in an endless battle between masculine and feminine, male and female, and same sex vs. hetero sexualities. Psychically it is suggested that we project our other half onto the opposite sex and enter into a psychological relationship of mirrors and reflections as a means of knowing ourselves. While this may be true, is it useful or even necessary?

From the perspective of a wholistic paradigm, each one of us contains the characteristics of masculine and feminine. Each one of us constitutes the whole. Spiritually we feel we are seeking completion in relationship, when in truth it is a matter of actualization. Relationship is the vehicle for this realization of the "I AM" individual.

Edgar Cayce and others suggest that we experience past lives, and that we keep coming back around, meeting each other again and again over numerous incarnations, each half seeking the other. When the accumulated karmic debt is cleared, the two will find one another, fuse back together, and return to the divine. So if one is not successful in finding an ideal mate, the lack of attainment may be explained as karma. "Not in this lifetime, it must be my karma." The idea is not to diminish the concept of karma, but to make conscious how this belief system operates in the culture and the personal psyche of an indvidual who may not even be aware of this belief. How does this spiritual belief, conscious or unconscious, affect and infect this life right here, right now?

How do we live with the symptoms that this concept implies? Are we incomplete until we fulfill our karmic debt, and then and only then do we find our soul mate? The seeker is kept in a state of paralysis, attempting perfection, with the hope of finding one's ideal mate. This unfortunate outcome hinders the individuation process which is dependent on the Self, the "I AM," for actualization.

The commitment to courtship allows us to attract someone who is also an individual. The synergy that lives between the two individuals serves as a catalyst to move us forward on the path. The revelation of divinity returns us to the "Holy Other" in relationship. Our sacred contract is renewed. Whatever the manner of our journey, alone or with another, it is a hallowed trust with the Divine. Our sacred contract is to awaken our potential towards actualization, to dissolve the boundaries and enter relationships with the intention for intimacy that will reveal and unfold itself in love, as love is our witness. And from this place we recognize the divine image, the divine ideal, the divine Love, Lover, and Beloved. We discover the true inner self of an individual, as opposed to the persona or outer aspect of the personality.

Gender as an Invention

There are two major areas of cultural splitting to address: the split between, indeed the war between, the sexes engineered through culturally created gender-based social identities and roles, and the psychospiritual split beween inner and outer experience, which is ultimately the split between self and other.

Pioneered by the women's liberation movement, we have come a long way in the last fifty years toward freedom from gender-based social identities, but we still have a long way to go. It is easy for those who have never experienced it to forget that women for thousands of years were considered bestial, filthy, evil, and impure by the patriarchal cultures which were the dominant cultures of the world; that women were kept in subjugation and humiliation as a normal part of most of the cultures of planet Earth; that women were "controlled by our parents until we are wives, then slaves to our husbands for the rest of our lives," as the folk song goes; that these are the cultural identities we have inherited, which we are in the long process of rebalancing at this time.

Biologically, the human embryo is neither male nor female for the first seven weeks of life. We begin gestation without sexual differentiation. Then the Y-chromosome triggers the production of testosterone, which promotes the development of male genetalia in some embryos. In the absence of this Y-chromosome, the embryo develops female genetalia. But there are vast genetic and hormonal variations among human beings. There is no factory-issue uniform male or female incarnation. In fact, we all remain inherently androgynous. We all produce both estrogen and testosterone, and our hormonal balances shift at different stages of life, as well as in response to the ever-changing environment we inhabit.

As contemporary social and sexual liberation proceeds, there is a corresponding disintegration and transformation of gender-based identities, along with that of conventional social and familial structures. Men and women are exchanging social roles and identities. Family structures are becoming more fluid. And a growing number of people are experiencing themselves as androgynous and/or bisexual and/or genderfluid. Men are no longer the sole breadwinners, the masters of external provision and survival. Women are no longer the sole nurturers, the mistresses of family and feelings. And it is no longer a given that men are on top of women socially, economically, sexually, or psychologically.

Psychology recognizes that men tend to have repressed feminine traits (the anima) and that women tend to have repressed masculine traits (the animus) and that these repressed traits can and are projected on to partners, so that the man sees the woman as representing and acting out his anima, and the woman sees the man as representing and acting out her animus. We cannot see each other clearly, let alone love each other truly, when we are caught in the hall of the mirror-like projections of our own unconscious psychic material on the other person. Becoming conscious of the unconscious and reclaiming our own masculine and feminine characteristics is a major element of a healthy relationship. At the same time we are coming to recognize that the animus and the anima and so many other psychic structures are the result of cultural conditioning and not inherent in the psyche. Growth to wholeness within ourselves and in relationship to others involves accepting and nurturing our own androgynous and genderfluid nature as well as allowing and loving androgyny and genderfluidity in our partners.

Conscious relationship with others is necessary in healing the split between inner and outer experience, between self and other. Conscious relationship begins by becoming ever more aware of one's own self, developing a healthy ego, an inner life, and a relationship between the ego and the Self, or the human and the divine. Through one's own personal confrontation, these dormancies, or places in the self seeking wholeness, are revealed, discovered, and accepted, and the Self is known. A deep self-searching reveals that the divine is fully present within us. Only by knowing and being firmly grounded in our own true nature can we have authentic love relationships with the true being of another. It takes One to know One.

At the same time, the inner life alone is not enough. The pitfalls of self-absorption, solipsism, and narcissism await the solitary seeker. Nothing can burn away the false self, the time-created neuroses, defenses, and addictions we all carry, like a true love relationship in tandem with constant inner work on one's self. A true love relationship with another is the divine in me loving the divine in a form other than my own, knowing that this other being's reality is equally as valid as my own reality and that we both come closer to Reality in our love together.

The myth of soul mates depicts completion by union with someone outside oneself, salvation through union with another person. We are suggesting continual courtship of the Beloved both in another person and within one's own Self simultaneously, for in Reality there is no separation between your Self and my Self. As Rumi sings, "Lovers don't finally meet somewhere. They're in each other all along."

Melancholy

"It was a quiet morning. I was reflecting on my life. I was happy in my marriage and career. I had all that I needed by way of material possessions and provision. I was drawn to my bedroom window and found myself staring out onto the sky, watching the white puffy clouds wisp along the horizon. The clouds veiled the light. All went gray. I experienced a strange emotion, heavy and deep with gloom. I was searching inside myself for something, yet I didn't know what it was. I was visited by a familiar feeling, a sense of melancholy. In the chambers deep in my heart lived an incessant longing — a holy longing. Unbeknownst to me, this moment of foreboding was a telling of a future that would come to pass. Within months my life as I knew it was completely deconstructed. And I was met by initiation into the path of love."

Symptoms of the Lost Art

So then what is all this restlessness? What is this feeling that something is missing, this wanting something more? What is that empty space a person experiences in his or her life? Is this due to the lack of courting? I have come upon several people in my practice who say they missed out on the courting experience during their adolescence, and who haven't experienced a "real" relationship until far into their mid-life. There is a valid truth to the vacancy they feel, because romance and love fulfill a spiritual desire. Want and hunger are religious activities of the psyche; they are necessary in order to gain a conscious awareness of the ontology, the nature of one's own being, for one's soul to awaken to its divinity. There is a natural intelligence carried by the impulse of our desires toward soulfulness, and we are driven to experience this in our relationships with others. By denying romance and sensuality, we nurture false states of security, which may fall into states of deep disillusionment, and the death of the courtship. Courting reveals spontaneous encounters and intrigue with the mystery of the other who so attracts you.

According to Aristotle, memory and imagination reside together in the soul. Emotional states ebb and flow in our being, causing deep, passionate currents to surface. It has to do with our inherent memory, and memory activates imagination. The heart remembers love. Love is a type of remembering that transports us to our divine connection. These symptoms are more severe in people who have lost their spiritual connection and lack a conscious relationship with the divine. They attempt to replace the divine with a relationship that lacks this intimacy, with an externalized and displaced "stand-in for the divine," someone who will heal them and love them, even take care of them.

Spirit is the vital principle or animating force within living beings. Melancholy, or feeling the blues, indicates an inner nostalgia, an insatiable desire, all of which are symptoms that arise as a result of separation, a lack of conscious experience of the divine. Melancholy is the depression of the spirit, accompanied by feelings of expulsion, of being lost and not knowing where one is. People feel anxious and lonely, and don't know how to keep themselves company. There is a sense of unexplainable distress. Melancholy is felt as a mysterious and silent desire, often with unknown origin. It is difficult to locate where the feeling is coming from because it has a transcendent quality, beyond present time and space. Often melancholy is described as "homesickness." Surges of unknown emotions and fantasies visit the realm of the imagination. One experiences waking dreamlike states, excessive images, palpable visions, and foresights which communicate where the soul is lacking. As we journey inwardly there is a numinous quality that pervades our desire. It is as if everything we have learned is no longer effective.

In the safety of one's private and intimate world, the work is to deconstruct and unlearn in order to know oneself. The voice of the Beloved draws you home. Her presence is ever more present. The call to awaken can be very spontaneous and disconcerting, and the journey back to the Self can be painful and difficult. For some this may be done in isolation, for others in the context of community; either choice is usually consistent with previous patterns for coping with pain.

In the evolution of the spiritual it is imperative to include the psychological. This is to avoid spiritualizing negativity and using spiritual teachings to by-pass neuroses and symptoms in need of deep psychological repair. Both spiritual and psychological practice, operating simultaneously, are optimal for the progress, safety, and realization of the individual.

Analysis involves self-inquiry and working with the unconscious. The depth approach is designed to access wounds, become conscious and restore oneself to the natural state. The goal of the work is to individuate and emerge as a Self, whole and complete. The more deeply one comes to confront, forgive, and discover the terrain of the psyche, the more a subtle transition occurs from personal to collective recognition. One is present and empathic toward human suffering. There is a cultivation of compassion toward oneself, which translates into compassion toward others and dissolves the illusions of separation. Our sameness is amplified. One connects with a greater wholeness of being, which includes human nature in all its diversity. Experienced on a continuum, an individual opens to states of deep acceptance and unity.

In the absence of personal work, the unexamined self is susceptible to illusive images of separation, commercial identities, and hypnotic states in a consumer-oriented reality. These states generate hunger, swarming desires, which keep us shopping. We go shopping for sex and food and products and procedures. Shopping — but what are you looking for? To appease the hunger, you eat and never get full. Or you talk with friends and hang up the phone, exhausted, but never satisfied. The "if onlys" set in... if only I could afford that new i-Phone... if only I could make more money... if only I could find... love.

Once we are done being filled by material possessions, food, and sex, what comes to dawn is a spiritual desire or hunger. The spiritual search begins, the search for a religion, a path, or a spiritual teacher. The process can take time, even years, and it is not unusual to encounter disappointment, frustration, regret, and despair. When one is worn out by this process, when all the options have been extinguished, when there are no more distractions, substitutes, or fillers, one comes up empty. There is a vast silence, a pregnant pause. When it seems like nothing is happening at all, everything is happening. What you yearn for is yearning for you. You are visited. The connection is visceral; it is holy, and the yearning subsides. The emotional turmoil simmers, and peace is made in union with the spiritual. There is a subtle transition to deep listening.

Longing is an indicator, a sign along the path of awakening. Love is the emotion propelling one to wholeness. And love is the source which comes from the divine. Fervent passion towards the lover, partner, and friend is the developing route to the ultimate relationship. Yearning is the desire to be whole and complete within one's Self. The journey goes through cycles that spiral up and down, down and up, all throughout a lifetime of psycho-spiritual development, eventually reaching beyond the personal to the transpersonal, to the spiritual attainment of an awakened soul. With every descent there is an ascent.

Eventually one moves from fleeting feeling to essence states, in which conscious awareness of oneself as a spiritual being takes hold and the core of oneself is strengthened. The false identities, the low self-esteem, the poor self-worth, the hurting, all gather around your sense of self, the ego, and begin to dissolve in the fire. One burns through darkness into light. The yearning and the burning is the Holy Spirit seeking to be realized. In this spiritual practice one loses oneself to find oneself. When you are fully engaged, the universe conspires with everything operating in your life, there is a consistent revelation of spiritual breakthroughs, magical moments, peak experiences, new wisdom, and a knowing that you are never alone, you are truly loved.

We come full circle. The erotic yearning of human love is the experience of divine love. The guiding passion dissolves boundaries and melts into ecstatic union. The dance of Love with the Lover as the Beloved is a search. It is the sacred art of courtship.

At the heart of every soul is longing for the sacred. Court the inner teacher, the spirit of guidance, the great spirit, the great goddess. Out of communion and dialogue a relationship is formed, courtship with the Holy Other. Separation is overcome not by the search for the other half, but by a deeper search, a spiritual search. Searching for a soul mate is an attempt to return and unite with the divine. The divine knows itself through separation, and the journey is to find itself in union. Longing transcends all the varieties of human love, and takes us to the Source.

The Soul Whole and Complete

The soul whole and complete is androgynous, hermaphroditic. And each soul, whole and complete, is individual and unique, so the psychosexual blend will be unique for each individual. As we move into the twenty-first century, there will be an increased evolution and reunion between the sexes. Two strict genders will become an archaic notion, birthed by mythologists who were duped by duality — a notion which diminishes the potential of a divinely whole and unified being.

Biologically the survival of the species is driven by the instinct to reproduce, but we all begin biological life androgynous. In the human embryo male and female genitals are identical for the first seven weeks of gestation. The same tiny knob of flesh becomes the clitoris in girls and the hooded head of the penis in boys. Although sexual differentiation determines gender, the consciousness of one sex remains.

In rites of initiation and passage in many societies it is common for the neophyte, the initiate, to be treated or represented as being neither male nor female, sexless as the soul is, or sometimes as being both male and female, androgynous as the soul is. The divine wants to experience itself in material creation, specifically in the human body, and be realized in the consciousness of humanity.

Chapter Four
Sexual History

Becoming One-self aggravates pre-existing structures, old models, and hierarchal institutions founded on superiority and inferiority. These models are incongruous with the growth and evolution of one's inner world. A seeker can no longer accommodate the status quo and is a stranger in one's own house, even one's marriage. In contemporary society today new forms of marriage emerge to accommodate the evolution of love and return us to sacred sexuality as a vehicle for awakening.

What is the point of all of this sex? The unconscious, rampant, anything and everything goes kind of sex? Is sex nothing more than blind lust, an instinct of the species, which uncontrolled produces AIDS and other sexually transmitted diseases, abortion, unwanted pregnancies, sexually abused children, over-population, and starvation of the masses?

Is this a testimony to a lack of awareness? Does sex need awareness and meaning?

How do we define our relationship to sex in the twenty-first century? How do we relate to our sexuality? Is there a social context for sex as pleasure and recreation, or does it remain reserved solely for the purpose of procreation? Is sex spiritual — and if so, to what purpose?

Is there a time to make our sex conscious, or cosmic and expansive enough to embody the participation of our own mystique and the making of a harmonious, erotic, and sensual world? Or should we just let it be... drive, lust, pulse, profane pleasure?

Sexual Evolution

In the early eras of humanity, the tribal roles of foraging and gathering were shared equally between the sexes. On all fours, females carried their young and hunted for food simultaneously along with the males. The shift in our sexual evolution began when we lifted ourselves off the ground and began walking on two legs. Carrying the infant with both arms affected the female's ablity to hunt independently. Furthermore, when females "stood up," they exposed their frontal body, lips, earlobes, breasts, and pelvic area, which in turn solicited visual attraction and face-to-face intimacy between the sexes. In response, male humans developed the largest penis of all the primates. Naturally females favored the males who were the strongest among the hunters and gatherers, thus guaranteeing the survival of their offspring. Sexual favors kept males from wandering off, keeping them close and provisionary.

Natural selection is the process by which the organisms best adapted to their environment tend to survive and transmit their genetic characteristics in increasing numbers to succeeding generations. Hence natural selection favors sexy females. Over the course of generations, sexually attractive females were the ones who prospered, along with strong, resourceful males, together producing healthy offspring.

Although pair-bonding and coupling was intended for the survival of the offspring, sex contracts were loose arrangements. The bond was not necessarily monogamous. Some males supported more than one female, and one female could pair with several males. For many, pair-bonding lasted only long enough for the mother to care for her young for the first four years. Then the couple would separate unless a second child was conceived. Curiously enough, approximately half the human population is genetically inclined toward sexual monogomy, explaining the ongoing phenomena of extra-marital liaisons, divorce, and serial monogamy.

Nonetheless, our ancestors set a precedent for what we call today marriage and family, as some such pair-bonds endured a lifetime of sexual monogomy, engendering yet another inter-generational prototype. Marriage, family, and sexual monogamy became the social standard of most societies.

Due to the "naturally selected" couples of our remote past, there is a genetic disposition in the culture for "family marriages," or two people who agree to intentionally come together to raise a family. In sync with the past, they often find themselves in a commitment crisis during the "empty nest," when the children leave home. When the task of raising the children self-completes, there is a natural tendency to move on. The couple is then confronted with redefining their roles in the relationship and the decision to re-commit to the marriage. A "family marriage" often finds itself revivified by the potential for grandchildren, reinforcing the bond and extending into the next generation.

However, youth today are gaining awareness about their reproductive rights and choices. Grandchildren are no longer a guarantee. Furthermore, divorce rates indicate that couples no longer wait until the children are grown to divorce. Divorced people seek new partners, reproduce with those partners, and co-produce blended family structures. In some cases, the initial marriage partner, male or female, is not sufficient in providing for the family, and the responsible parent, who by now may have several children and sex appeal, attracts a fit and equal provider who is geared toward family and is happy to participate and even reproduce in the pre-existing family unit.

Troops to tribes, tribes to clans, clans to extended family systems, which separate to nuclear families, and by division and divorce remarry and reproduce blended families — it takes a village to raise this tribe. Familial singles with children attract pair-bonding singles. Singles who can't find a mate have resourced the ability to self-inseminate, reproduce, and give birth. The Western trend in the twenty-first century includes marital constancy, nuclear families, serial monogamy, blended families, and/or group marriage.

The notion of one father or one mother is rapidly becoming an outdated idea. More and more people don't get hung up over the fact that they have both had sexual relations with the same person. They are all involved in raising the children and co-depending on each other's resources to provide for their needs. The parents are primarily responsible, but all the new partners that come into the tribe/village are emotionally responsible, and thus develop a different kind of nurturance and intimacy. Hence, one parent may be good at the economic and the next at the emotional, which can compensate for the lack existing in the first marriage.

Some people suffer because they have natural tendencies which are inclined to prevail over cultural mores and expectations. Although they have sincerely tried to "make their marriage work," an innate impulse to move on produces intense inner conflict. Seeking therapy is not unusual at this juncture. Their concern is that there is something wrong with them because they just can't make their marriage work, compared to their other friends and family. There is a sorrow that lives in their hearts, laden with guilt and shame. Their issue is not necessarily psychological but rather biological. They feel "different" and indeed they are. They are genetically inclined towards different roles as a result of their ancient ancestry. They are separate from a culture whose reward systems cultivate personalities that dominate over natural human tendencies. This is not an issue of "nature or nurture" but rather of "culture over nature."

Half the population carries in their genes the DNA to remain married and faithful, while the other half of the population is a unique potpourri of coupling dispositions, spreading and enhancing those genes. This is the result of ancient reproductive strategies used by both sexes, residing in the primitive patterns of the DNA. Males notoriously engage in extra-marital trysts, spreading their genes, and self-replicating a future flock. Women choose one male, then sexually engage with a "special friend" to acquire additional resources. The activity of extra-marital affairs leads to divorce. Unbeknownst to most of us, the human population has been participating in an ancient reproductive game. In addition, we have an emerging spiritual population with a disposition toward the life eternal, rather than the fear of our own genetic death. We also share a spiritual ecology which, by reducing the use and consumption of natural resources, supports the planet to sustain future generations. For some of us this also means refraining from reproducing.

Thus, the old and new generations of children carry forth the genetic blueprint and brain chemistry for marriage, divorce, and remarriage, which is the most common love style in the US today. This is serial monogamy, in which pairing with a new partner follows after a divorce — a form of monogamy in which participants have only one sexual partner at any one time, but have more than one sexual partner in their lifetimes. Partners can be married or unmarried, but there is never more than one partner at a time. Within Western culture this form of monogamy is more prevalent than true monogamy, which is having only one partner in an entire life. The momentum of serial monogamy erodes the cultural models of family and marriage, and bids us to expand our horizons towards acceptable alternatives for both partners. In a rapidly changing world, we are seeking a coupling that is compatible with our ancient human spirit and does not preclude sacred sexuality.

The Sacred Sack

"I always knew that sex was sacred. Contrary to my thinking, everyone I knew was just having sex for the sake of sex. After years of sex, fun, and monogamy, I continued to feel dissatisfied. Something was missing. As I got older, my early inclinations grew potent. I just knew that sex was a vehicle for two people to experience something divine. I wonder how many of us know our sex is sacred and we just don't have the words for it. I was nearly thirty years old when I found someone who knew about sexual love. She said, 'Oh you're talking about high sex. You are describing the art of sexual ecstasy. Some call it the Tantra, by which the lovers, masculine and feminine, dissolve in the One.'

"I remember the first time I encountered my sacred lover.... He came to me, and all I could do was smile. He looked at me and said, 'You are such a joyful lover!'"

Sacred Sexuality

Sacred sex shifts the emphasis from procreation to sacred ecstasy. Sacred sex is a vehicle for conscious co-creation and union with the Divine in each of us and through one another — sexual experience as spiritual harmony that attends to our sexual nature, human ecology, and divine inheritance.

Sexual pleasure and intimacy lead to bonding, which under constancy forms emotional attachments which endure over time. When the motive evolves beyond the practical application of sex, the venue is open to explore beyond the personal towards the transpersonal. Our perception of our ancient sexual ancestry goes from the scientific and biological to a sentient and evolving consciousness.

In certain cultural and spiritual traditions, sex is considered sacramental. Both men and women engage in intercourse as spiritual communion. For the devout, sex is an integral part of religion. The motive has nothing to do with payment, survival, or exchange, rather with a desire to experience intimate contact with the divine.

Sacred sex is modeled in the Jewish Shabbat ritual, where it is a mitzvah for the husband to make love to his wife on the Sabbath. According to the Zohar, when two people make love it is a re-enactment of the mystery of Union: "just as the male and female aspects of the Divine unite above, so they also unite below in the mystery of the Oneness." Some understand this as a sensual whisper from Adonai on the Sabbath calling husbands and wives to weave the dance of sex as an act of worship, their passions mirroring the divine male and female aspects of the Creator. Each caress in this unhurried tryst echoes the love of the Creator for the Creation.

Taoist sages have taught for nearly five thousand years that intercourse assists in longevity and union with the cosmos. Sexual union between the yin and yang, the masculine and feminine principles, maintains balance between complementary forces, Heaven-Male and Earth-Female. Through intercourse there is union between Heaven (which rains sperm) and Earth (the ova) which gives life to all things.

In the Hindu tradition the Supreme Being is both male and female, with the qualities of both genders. Intercourse is identified with mystical union, where boundaries between the sexes are blurred, leading to an intense spiritual experience. Each woman and man embodies the qualities of both male and female. And during intercourse, when both are merged, they join with the Absolute, itself of no defined gender.

Sacred sexuality is an aspect of Hindu and Buddhist Tantric traditions. Tantrism depicts images of deities copulating with goddesses. For tantrics copulation involves the imitation of this divine pairing between God and Goddess, which generates continuous waves of orgasmic cosmic energy circulating between the lovers, making the natural supernatural and producing states of infinite ecstasy and bliss. In that state of bliss the one lover reveals the reality of the other lover. In consciousness and through the body, Bliss touches emptiness. In the shared breathing a true rhythm comes into being where the love-making happens as if by itself. Then it is all turned around: love is making us, rather than we who are trying to make love. Love opens us to states of non-duality, wholeness, and glints of enlightenment. This love opens out everywhere, radiating peace, warmth, and clarity.

In the ancient alchemical tradition, the masculine Sol (Sun) and feminine Luna (Moon) undergo a series of alchemical processes that evolve and develop through the conjunctio (joining together), which evolves into the two melding into the One in the consciousness of the divine and the attainment of the Holy Marriage, *Hieros Gamos*.

There is no denying our collective memory of sacred sex. The spiritual conception redefines the identity of human intercourse. We don't have to necessarily adopt these belief systems as our own, but rather consider the incorporation of the spiritual dimension into our own sexuality — sex as a mystical engagement that produces union with the divine, the Absolute, the One, spiritual Bliss.

Chapter Five
The Biology and Chemistry of Love

Spiritual depth and connection to the Beloved activates one's erotic nature. As a seeker dives into the erotic dimension, the libidinal drive is liberated. Libido matched with spiritual desire gives way to sexual energy, the life force, which creates and generates hunger for union. As in courtship, to experience the ultimate fulfillment and purpose of this life energy requires patience and concentration. It is not necessary that a Lover abstain from sexual love, but to approach the experience in tandem with a spiritual consciousness. Courtly love is arrested by misappropriating spiritual desire for sexual hunger. Sex is split off from love and love is split off from sex, promoting unnecessary pain and suffering, as well as self-defeating sexual habits. One gets lost in the boiling cauldron of erotic sexual dialogues and dalliances. It is imperative while exploring the erotic terrain to navigate bio-chemical encounters that appear in the guise of spiritual reunions.

Through all the stages of courtship we have a natural tendency towards love, bonding, and attachment, characteristics which parallel the spiritual path and our relationship with the Divine. If we deny, ignore, or are too quick to move to intimacy, we miss out on the natural progression toward trust and rapport.

Courtship is a formality which allows the couple to determine their likenesses, attraction, and values. Within a few meetings, two people can determine if they hold a similar picture or different visions and goals regarding relationship. It can be very helpful to first define the type of relationship you are seeking. Within the first couple of weeks of courting, you can experience how a person is going to be in a relationship based on how they behave. For example, one or the other party is generous or tight with money; one or the other calls or doesn't call when they say they will; one or the other is passive and tentative about moving forward, or aggressive and eager to make the date permanent.

Courting has a biological component, which are built-in mechanisms that screen whether or not there is genuine compatibility toward a love interest. How is psyche informing our chemistry and how does biology inform our psyche? Body and psyche are interrelated. Behaviors produce emotions and emotions produce behaviors. Without progressing and evolving a relationship with a love interest, the opportunity for healthy functional development is absent, and people find themselves on an emotional roller coaster ride — especially people who are operating from sexual attachment. The human heart not only becomes exhausted by the sex, it is also depleted by the lack of love.

Although love is a subjective experience, there are behaviors and signs that culminate as actions which can be scientifically observed. Intimate connections are verbal, visual, and sensual, expressed through touching and physical contact.

What joins us with the rest of the universe is that we form attachment and strong bonds with one another, parents, siblings, friends, and sexual partners. When there is a lack of experience and nurturing contact, unhealthy or no attachment is formed. Our brains hold a natural potential for falling in love — and when it is not being fulfilled in the relationship, without warning one may seek to create a bond outside the "official one." Couples who form marriages for conventional social reasons often compensate for the lack of love in the marriage by seeking love outside the marriage to fulfill their emotional needs.

In our world today there are couples who benefit from a traditional marriage model. Yet for others the traditional models of relationship do not work. Anthropologist Desmond Morris provides a well-researched framework for those seeking a pair-bonded experience, and addresses the "biology of love." Helen Fisher's revolutionary work on the "chemistry of love" addresses the scope of "love types," providing answers for those who don't adapt to a traditional model.

The Biology of Love

Courtship is a process by which the initial attraction between two people develops into rapport and trust over time, increasing intimacy and allowing lovers to form as a pair. As with so many of the species in the wild kingdom, humans also undergo patterns of courtship, with typical sequences in the course of a love affair. Each stage takes the relationship to a new threshold, passing and moving us to the next, producing the foundation for the development of love and pair bonding. It is no wonder that people who do not take the time to court and develop the relationship often break off abruptly, leaving one or the other dissatisfied and emotionally wounded. Courtship is a process by which a couple can develop intimacy within the nature of instinctual sensibility while participating in the phases, stages, and thresholds of the coupling process. The various stages and thresholds of courtship serve as a guideline and invitation for the lost in love.

There are subtle forms of contact that suggest movement toward or dismissal of a potential mate. We use our eyes to make contact, we listen to each other's voices, we sense smells, we dabble in touch, and, if we remain interested, we engage in physical body-to-body contact and deeper sexual intimacy.

First encounters are visual assessments and determine attraction or repulsion. Within seconds another person determines whether or not you are attractive based on your sex, age, size, status, skin color, and mood. If the attraction is present, each person takes turns looking at the other, eye-to-eye. Walking past each other and turning to meet each other's glance with a smile indicates an interest or mutual attraction. If the responses are not returned, the two stop and go no further. This is a significant cue. If you're not interested, refrain from response. Don't feel sorry for the person or flatter yourself by being kind to them if you're genuinely not interested. Otherwise you may be entering into unconscious territory, overriding your healthy instinctual response which is, "I don't find that person attractive." Rather than trusting instinct, you may find yourself attracted by another's attraction to you and allow yourself to be seduced.

For many the initial attraction is enough cause for two people to take each other to bed. Casual sex promotes relating to each other's image or fantasy, and lacks the intimacy of emotionally relating to a person. Generally these encounters are short-lived or wrought with drama and misunderstandings. The courtship itself is short-circuited and lacks the necessary time for emotional development.

Given a mutual attraction, yet withholding from physical contact, the couple proceeds to the next stage of courtship. The initial stage of attraction ranges from seconds to months, with one potential partner silently admiring the other from a distance. Watching and observing builds mystery and a silent erotic enticement. Don't let it go on for too long. If you're interested, move it forward and strike up a conversation.

It is prudent to keep initial conversations in the realm of small talk, and to meet in public environments for short periods of time. To operate in this modality clearly acknowledges that the two are in the beginning stages of intimacy. There is an opportunity to engage each other through conversation and determine if they feel nurtured, interested, and mutually pleased by the discussions. These are indicators that the couple is capable of effective communication. Voice-to-voice contact is another screening device that determines attraction. When we hear each other's voice, the brain immediately reads the level of intelligence based on the vocabulary, street smarts, or educated speech. If the voice is irritating or lacks mutual intelligence, interest is withdrawn.

All too often when two people find themselves mutually attracted and turned on by the voice, they disclose and share their entire life history too quickly and get very personal with someone who is essentially a stranger or mere acquaintance. It's as if you are their long-standing friend. Because the attraction is a powerful connection, each one assumes the other knows what they are talking about, disclosing things before an agreement for future courting has been decided. I call this type of immediate deep disclosure "false intimacy." Two people are brand new in their encounters and they bombard each other with their life stories, problems, and relationship profiles. It is unconscious relating, and overrides the opportunity for two people to get to know each other, or for one or the other to withdraw from the courtship.

People engaging in false intimacy run the risk of being emotionally manipulated into an instant intimate connection that in the long run has no substance. Voice, vibration, attraction, and contact are very important instinctual indicators, and may prove your interest unattractive despite your initial visual signal.

Avoid being discouraged. Rather be encouraged by the evidence for or against proceeding with an individual. This allows you to move into or on to a relationship that holds the potential you are seeking. Give yourself the opportunity to court. It allows you to stop and withdraw before it turns into something you really don't want. More and more people go against their natural instincts.

As two people agree to move forward in their courtship, the potential for non-sexual touch increases. If this is unwelcome by either party, the relationship goes no further. When it is invited, non-sexual touch can come in the form of greeting, brushing up against an arm, or assisting one another physically. That first physical touch can feel like a spark, even electric. And if you don't like how it feels to be even non-sexually touched, too soft, too aggressive or hungry... take notice. The tendency to move forward is present when both people are expressing a mutual desire. Physical contact may progress to putting arms around each other and drawing closer, with arms around each other's waists.

One of the most erotic and enticing moments, which is clearly underrated, is the first kiss. The kiss, face to face, is a full frontal embrace. This initial moment produces physiological response and arousal, leading a person to experience sexual excitement, genital tingling, moistness, and erection. The first kiss may include stroking and smelling each other's hair, touching the ears, head, neck, and face.

In the post-kissing phase, hands wander and discover each other's bodies, fondling, massaging, and exploring the other's physical landscape. It can be very helpful for you to know what gives you pleasure, to encourage and cue your partner when their touch makes you feel good. Lack of response leads to aimless wandering. It can also be helpful to communicate your desires. But be aware — some lovers take offense if they are sexually immature and their egos bruise easily.

Let your partner know your pleasure zones: your back, your belly, the soles of your feet — "Oh yes, touch me there." It enhances future foreplay and is central to a positive and mutually satisfying experience. Partners experience increasing arousal — and often this may be where they stop. Arousal is powerful. If one or the other is hesitant, tentative, uncomfortable, and yet allows deeper physical contact, it makes it more difficult to stop and break away from the relationship and may give way to emotional conflict. "I'm not sure I really like this person" — "but this sure feels good." Stop, regroup, and revisit your level of interest. Be emotionally honest with yourself.

Without the development of mutual trust, it is best that advanced sexual intimacy is postponed. When mutual trust is established and both parties continue and agree to further exploration, the couple enters into the realm where there is a need for a private sensual environment.

At the risk of sounding pedantic, it is important to ask your partner about sexually transmitted disease. I have been forever fascinated by the fact that we take off our clothes and expose our bodies and yet find it impossible to ask these questions. Asking allows you to make conscious decisions and take appropriate and safe measures to ensure a positive sexual outcome. I am sorry if the last person you slept with didn't tell you, but simply put: two wrongs don't make it right. Inquiry as to the health of each other's bodies indicates that you care about yourself and your partner. It is mature and considerate to be aware. More times than not, if there is a sexually transmitted disease between you there are simple measures and remedies. Honest disclosure aligns you and begins the relationship with sexual integrity. In fact, disclosure heightens the trust and bonding between two people. Keep it conscious.

In the privacy of a quiet environment, you learn how to play— through foreplay you explore pleasurable ways of stimulating each other preceding intercourse by touching and enjoying different sensations. Sucking each other's breasts promotes arousal and activates the desire for climax. Hands caress and stimulate the genitals. Oral sex pleasures one another to orgasm. If this is unfamiliar territory, pick up a couple of books on foreplay and learn how to bring your partner to orgasm through manual and oral stimulation. Most people don't know what or where a clitoris lives, let alone endless erotic ways of stimulating a penis. Books on sexual positions and possibilities are valuable resources, especially if you want to take your time and create heightened states and alternative experiences of awareness in your love-making.

Mutual orgasmic experience serves as a good precursor to healthy sexual intercourse between lovers. For the female, her ability to reach an orgasm is directly correlated with a refined awareness of her partner's care towards her. The development of intimacy and contact, trust and sexual satisfaction, creates a deeper bond. When this is undeveloped and premature, it is not unusual to move on to another lover once orgasm has been reached.

In each phase there is a deeper intimacy cementing the bond, taking the couple further in their sexual exploration. Before you go further, please sit down and discuss planned parenting. Explore your values regarding pregnancy, abortion, and post-abortion syndrome, and the use of all the varieties of birth control available to both men and women, from natural rhythmic methods to the morning-after pill. Partners who want to be great lovers take time to explore the different stages of sexual intimacy and gain the confidence for the final stage of courtship… making love.

In the modern culture of quick gratification it is not atypical for two people to meet, have sex, and, if there is an interest or a sexual bond, remain in the relationship even when their instincts know better. "Hooking up" is a popular phrase used by the teen and college culture to define casual and exploratory sex. Although this is the initial agreement between parties, recent research indicates that fifty percent of people hooking up hoped to trigger long-term relationships; of these only one-third met with success, and depression arose in those that did not achieve a long-term relationship. Thus, if your intention goes beyond random sexual engagement, courting a partner prior to sexual sampling is conducive. The uniqueness of a conscious courtship, by which two people agree to get to know each other over a period of time, is that it is free of sexual attachment and allows the couple to disengage if the pairing is unsatisfactory.

Pheromones

Body odor plays a powerful role in sexual attraction. Pheromones secreted in our sweat, especially in our armpits, serve as signals to the most primitive part of the brain, the limbic system. The most primitive of the senses is the sense of smell. The limbic system governs our most basic drives, such as thirst, hunger, fear, rage, and sexual arousal, all of which profoundly influence our emotions, memory, and creativity.

The word *pheromone* comes from Greek words which mean stimulus (*hormone*) and transporter (*pherein*), i.e., "excitement carrier." Our pheromones are our unique "smell prints" which are as individual as fingerprints. They communicate attraction or repulsion to the deepest part of our awareness. Studies suggest that pheromones communicate sexual attraction to mates who are not genetically similar, whose immune systems differ from our own, and who have different biological vulnerabilities than we have, increasing the likelihood of stronger, healthier children. Pheromones in bodily secretions stake our claim and mark another person as our territory.

The odor of the other communicates all sorts of information that either produces instinctual caution or intense attraction. Trust your sense of smell. If another person smells good to you, they may very well be good for you. And if you instinctively dislike the way they smell, don't let yourself go any further. Do you still like the way they smell after six months of being together? If not, you'd better pack your bags. And beware of the masking of perfumes and colognes, including the artificial pheromones that are widely sold. You want to love the real smell of the au naturel body of your lover. Your imagination may run wild with all sorts of confusing infatuations, but your sense of smell will not lead you astray.

You Might as Well Face It, You're Addicted to Love

"I can't tell you how many hours I spent on the phone with friends, and how much money I spent on shrinks. No one knew what to do.... There was no psychological, spiritual, or emotional explanation for being with this woman. It

was as if I were in a trance. I would just find myself going to her and holding on to the relationship and yet I didn't even really like her. I would get such a rush when I had sex with her. I didn't want to give her up. Her love was my drug. One therapist told me, 'If you could just have enough sex with her, you could get her out of your system.' This went on for seven years! I ended up engaged and almost married to her! In the long run the only thing that cut the cord was to stop having sex with her — extreme circumstances and intense withdrawal. Even after I broke it off numerous times, I would find myself going back for more. After a final breakup I remained vulnerable, never knowing if I could withstand her. I feared the day I would run into her again. Nearly five years later I came upon some revolutionary research on love types and brain chemistry. Dr. Fisher's work enabled me to finally reach a resolution and gave me the strength to resist that temptation. It saved my life."

The Chemistry of Love

Modern courtship has gone "from the front porch to the back seat," from courting to going steady to dating to hooking up. Two people get together to mess around, to make out, and to have sex with no strings attached. Casual sex, careless love, and "friends with benefits" are becoming more and more the norm. Let's have sex first and maybe get to know each other — or not — later. Sex as fun, sex as recreation, is all fine if you're into it, even though it can lead to sex as consumption and addiction. The invisible vulnerability is that physical sex generates passionate attachment chemicals in the body, and you can end up feeling strongly bonded to someone you barely know, someone with whom you have not taken the time to find out how emotionally (or intellectually, socially, or spiritually) compatible you are. You may find yourself "joined at the hip" to someone who makes your life miserable, either by clinging to you or breaking up with you and leaving you chemically (and emotionally) bereft. This can be confusing, not to say devastating, especially for a young soul just getting to know itself.

Modern research in the fields of the biochemistry and neurophysiology of love, pioneered by Dr. Helen Fisher, a biological anthropologist, gives an illuminating perspective on the power and paradoxes of human sexuality. The biological purpose (not the spiritual, pleasurable, or ecstatic purpose) behind all sexual activity is the reproduction of the species. The intelligence within life has created powerful instinctual drives and irresistible neurological pleasures in the body to ensure that this purpose is fulfilled.

Dr. Fisher proposed that there are three core brain systems governing sexual attraction, mating, and consequent reproduction. These three neurological pathways govern respectively lust, attraction, and attachment. Lust is the sex drive, sexual heat, libido, the craving for simple sexual gratification. Attraction is romantic love, falling in love, the urge to merge, with all of the emotional intensity involved. Attachment is settling into the comfort and stability of a long term relationship. These roughly correspond to anthropologist Desmond Morris's stages of courtship: mating, pair bonding, and parenting. All three stages together insure that conception and birth take place and that the parents stay together long enough to raise the child, ensuring the survival of the species.

The underlying neurological paradox is that while these three brain systems are separate and independent (although related) neurological pathways, they evolved together and are connected. These three activities can and do operate either simultaneously and/or independently of each other, often at the same time. One person is biologically capable of being stabilized in marriage (attached) to one person while being totally in love with (attracted to) another person while at the same time having sex (lust) with whoever is available at the moment — and/or experiencing all three love activities with the same person.

Lust is driven by the levels of androgens and estrogens, male and female hormones, in the bloodstream. Different individuals have differing levels of these sex hormones, resulting in varied levels of sex drives, according to constitution and age. Popular wisdom has it that women peak at 40, men at 18, a meaningful generality perhaps, but one that cannot be applied to specific persons. Eventually the levels of sex hormones decline with age. Estrogen levels increase in men and testosterone levels increase in women after midlife. Lust by itself is easily, if temporarily, gratified by sexual release, and can be relatively impersonal, playing out in anonymous sex and one-night stands.

Lust drives us to experience a variety of partners. At the same time lust brings us into close contact with other human beings. Lust is often the gateway to a deeper attraction.

Passionate romantic love is characterized by intense feelings, high energy levels, sleeplessness, loss of appetite, focused attention, obsessive thinking, and intense craving for the object of this love. The heart is racing, giddy, awake, and alive. There are profound mood swings, ranging from euphoria and ecstasy to depression and hopelessness. These are due to the chemicals the brain is releasing: dopamine, norepinephrine, and phenylethylamine. Functional magnetic resonance imaging of lovers looking at the image of their beloved showed increased blood flow to areas of the brain with high concentrations of receptors for dopamine, which produces pleasure, euphoria, and craving for more, stimulating a biological drive to attach to one other person. Norepinephrine stimulates adrenaline production, which causes elevated heart activity, heightened awareness, sleeplessness, and hyperactivity. Phenylethylamine, which is similar in structure to amphetamines, produces a feeling of ecstasy. In addition, some researchers have found lower levels of serotonin in people in love, as are found in people with obsessive-compulsive disorders, explaining why people in love tend to obsess about their love object.

Then when people have sex, oxytocin is released in both sexes during orgasm. Oxytocin is the pleasurable "cuddling chemical" which produces bonding between sex partners. The more orgasmic the sex, the greater the bonding. The body also produces vasopressin, a hormone associated with long-term bonding and monogamy. In addition, endorphins, the body's natural opiates, are involved in the longevity of love, as they have pain-killing and pleasure-giving properties.

The intensity of passionate love fades after two or three years. It is believed that the ascendancy of the bonding chemicals (oxytocin and vasopressin) interfere with the neural pathways for the passion chemicals (dopamine, norepinephrine, and phenylethylamine). The obsessive attraction to, craving for, and idealization of the other begin to subside (emotionally as well as chemically) and the calm, peace, and stability of a long-term relationship comes forth. Attachment grows as passion fades. Long-term attachment allows parents to cooperate in raising children. This state is characterized by feelings of calm, security, social comfort and emotional union.

Some people become addicted to the intensity and drama of the passion chemicals and cannot stay in a stable relationship once the height of passion has faded. They crave the high of being in love with one after another. However, the body builds up a tolerance for the passion chemicals and as time goes along the love junky needs greater and greater stimulation to achieve the same high. There is a term for this: love-and-sex addicts — except now we know there are biochemical processes in the body that produce these effects. Having all the sex in the world, in the absence of romantic passion or the comfort of bonding, can become a depleting and even dangerous addiction. On the other hand, couples in long term relationships have the challenge of keeping the sex and the romance (excitement) alive, and not being smothered in cuddling chemicals.

We have different brain systems that work separately and independently of one another. One can feel lust towards one person, deep attraction toward another, and attachment to yet another. Each type of love involves different felt experiences, which in turn activate different neurotransmitters and chemical/hormonal releases in the brain. The symptoms range from sexual arousal driven by androgens and estrogens, to passion and romance which release the exciting passion chemicals in the body, to the comfort and security of bonded attachment created by oxytocin and vasopressin. The dynamic interplay of these three brain systems generate the glory, the heartbreak, and the perplexing complexity of the human love experience, ranging from romantic comedy to downright tragedy.

How can you be committed to and love your partner and crave to have sex with your friend next door? The sight of her hot body ignites the brain, which then in turn activates hormones that spark these desires. What about the bad boys and naughty girls? You know better, yet they are like magnets with excess amounts of testosterone and estrogen. No matter how hard you try to win their love or want them to bond to you, forget it, folks. They are tormenting, moody, and violent. They marry less and divorce more.

What about the lovers who don't want you when you're single, but only when you are bonded to someone else? Herein lies a mystery. They can crave emotional highs and passionate escapades, but they are incapable of bonding. Your wedding ring takes the pressure off of them. You're already bonded to someone else, so it's safe to have sex without the possibility of involvement, or so they think.

Watch out for those love interests that come your way with whom you just want to have sex and nothing else. After a couple of sexual experiences that are orgasmic and satisfying you find yourself falling in love with someone with whom you could never have imagined a long-term relationship. Because the sex is so incredible, you find yourself wanting more. It's not necessarily because you want them, but the influences of oxytocin and vasopressin chemically and emotionally bond you to them. Stop sleeping with them now. Refrain from any further coitus. Otherwise you could find yourself walking down the aisle and asking yourself, "How did I get here?" Stay out of bed with people you don't want to get involved with long term — or know that you are taking a risk. And lastly, trust your crash when they leave you and thank the heavens you are free to move on and find a more suitable partner.

What about the types with whom you have a lot of honeymoon sex and simultaneous orgasms? Remember those lovers: they are "partner material" — and the hardest to get over if they seek that next love high. The passion and romance hormones subside after two or three years and the hormonal pathways that keep that rush happening are railroaded by the bonding hormones that settle us down into the routine of life together. Be careful: you can bond and attach, but no telling for how long you can stand to cuddle on the couch, eat and sleep together, and make a commitment to be monogamous, unless you intentionally keep the fire of passion alive through erotic play, date nights, and romantic vacations. Even good sex can become routine.

And what about the people who get married and never experience love, passion, attachment, and bonding? Some of those who report they have never felt romantic love suffer from hypopituitarism, a rare disease in which the pituitary malfunctions in infancy, causing hormonal problems as well as love blindness. These men and women lead normal lives, some even marry for companionship, but that rapture, that heartache, of passionate love is mythology to them.

In your own sexual and evolutionary development, there may be a tendency to experience one hormonal encounter after another. And you still haven't found what you're looking for… until sexual orgasm and emotional love are experienced in the same relationship. Sex and love are characterized by a sense of merger and heightened states of transcendent awareness.

Love is about more than just genes. Bonding is about more than just biology. Cultural and social factors play large roles. Who and how a person has loved in the past are important determinants of his/her capacity to fall in love at any given moment in the future. This is because animals, people included, learn from their sexual and social experiences. Arousal comes naturally. But long-term success in mating requires a change from being naïve to being aware of the precise factors that lead from arousal to the rewards of sex, love, and attachment. Studies indicate that the longer the courtship, the stronger the long-term relationship. So if you are interested in having a long-term relationship, take your time and experience a courtship that will support endurance.

Can passion last in long-term relationships? It is possible to trick the brain into feeling romantic love in a long-term relationship by doing novel things with your partner. Any arousing activity drives up the level of dopamine and can therefore trigger feelings of romance as a side effect. Date nights, holidays, and vacations can keep passion alive.

If you are just not interested, or are operating out of other love types and chemical influences, define yourself and enjoy. Just keep in mind that not all lovers can make the transition to become steady, stable, relationships. Some lover types can only exist in the bedroom chamber and cannot make a transition from the lover to the bonder. If the connection is lust- and sex-driven, then it is likely you will be in the loop for lovers only. The engagement with the lover eventually aborts for those seeking secure reproductive territory.

Chapter Six
Love in the Twenty-First Century: Alternative Models and Trends

Courting the Beloved is a personal journey which enacts a universal theme. The Lover encounters the Self through experiences, mistakes, repetitions of love, in all her many forms. Life in love is no longer one's own. Grace rises and assigns love to something beyond the self. As the aspirant withdraws his or her energies from outer world and connects with the divine impulse of love, he/she experiences a true revelation: courtship is a journey in God. One unites with the Beloved in permanent possession of a divine identity. Union awakens Lovers to serve in the world. Individuated couples, operating in communion, function as a sacred trinity.

The institution of marriage has been the foundation of social and economic stability in one form or another in virtually every human society. Though some societies in some time periods allowed love attraction to play a significant role in the formation of marriages, by and large marriages have been arranged and approved by families to preserve and enhance bloodlines, wealth and property, cultural and religious values, and provide a stable container for bringing forth offspring. Spontaneous sexual attraction and romantic love have been seen as dangers to the institution of marriage — or alternatively as temporary release valves for the instinctual drives not met in a marriage.

The women's liberation movement has been perhaps the greatest catalyst for social change in the past hundred years. And the change is far from over, affecting every area of life, as women gain equality in education, in employment, in politics, in the family, in the bedroom, and in the boardroom. Increasingly women have the right to uphold the integrity of their own bodies and minds, in particular the right and ability to decide whether or not they wish to conceive a child at any given time, leading to an era of unprecedented sexual freedom that challenges the institution of marriage. Traditional marriage will continue to be a good choice for pair-bonding and child-rearing, but it is no longer the only choice, and less and less is it necessarily a life-long choice.

Sixty years ago child abuse, sexual abuse, and rape were underreported, rarely successfully prosecuted, and bore significant stigma for the victims. Divorce was on the rise, but was still socially devastating for the divorced woman. Divorce was an option for men alone to exercise. Homosexual males and females generally had to keep a low profile and lead "normal" lives without acknowledging their sexual orientation. Cross-dressers had to confine themselves to their wives' closets. The concept of transgender was unknown. Sex was simply not talked about publicly. Philandering, adultery, and extra-marital affairs went on, as they have in all ages, but under the cloak of male authority and male supremacy. What was good for the gander was not permitted for the goose.

Women's liberation brings sexual liberation for both males and females, liberation from oppression, suppression, and hypocrisy. We are not trading the oppression of women for the oppression of men — we are upgrading. Women are responsible for this historic change through education, birth control, economic value, and social equality. Women are the ones who are making this change. At the same time it is important for women to realize that it is women who shape the future of relationship. Now it is up to women to determine the usefulness or uselessness of a marriage. It is now possible and desirable for women to walk away from a stagnant, abusive, lack-love marriage.

In the 1960's it appeared as if society was making a shift and sexual pleasure would become the ground for love and commitment. There were high expectations put on the sex life. When marriages were measured against this single standard, couples found themselves in marital disillusionment, which often became the ground for divorce. The standard set by the marriage suffocated the erotic dimension of the courtship.

When we look at marriage today in America, we find we are moving from the traditional "gender role marriage" to the "companionate marriage." In the companionate marriage, husband and wife each have a career, and they co-parent and co-housekeep according to the gender-free norms they negotiate. We hold two values at once: a culture of marriage and a culture of individualism. This is the new war between the sexes: "I want my independence and I want to have you, too." Independence, sexual frustration, discontent, and restlessness result in an increase of women initiating divorce. America is both a marriage culture and a divorce culture — we both marry and divorce at some of the highest rates anywhere on the globe. We need to shift our core values from traditional marriage to domestic stability. The harm in single parenthood comes from the single parent continually coupling with new partners, where children are forced to bond or compete for attention, with "ever new mates."

Along with women's liberation, there are three main influences that have changed the face of marriage in the post modern era: birth control, reproductive technology, and life expectancy. Birth control and reproductive choices freed sexuality and child-birthing from the confines of marriage. Not only did birth control free everyone to experiment and explore sexuality without the consequence of pregnancy, it also gave us the option not to reproduce. This is amazing. It means that people who are not meant to be parents no longer have to force themselves to comply. People can choose to get married for love, for sex, for companionship, for fun, and not have to reproduce. As we move our attention from the progeneration of the species to the generation of our personal potential, the concentration shifts from the external to the internal, forcing couples to examine themselves and each other as well as the relationship.

A childless marriage challenges the tradition that the central purpose of marriage is to bear children, just as much as gay couples having children challenges the exclusivity of the one-man-one-woman marriage. Now that gay, lesbian, and bisexual people and couples are coming out of the closet, they too are demanding that their unions be recognized as equal with traditional marriages in terms of sanctity, civil rights, social status — and the right to have children.

We are in the thick of a reproductive revolution. A woman who can't find a husband but wants a baby goes to the sperm bank and has her womb inseminated. A gay man who wants children can pay a surrogate mother to be inseminated with his seed and carry his offspring. Likewise, a surrogate mother can carry an inseminated egg for another woman. Men and women can have their fertility enhanced, enabling them to overcome natural limitations. Men and women can have their tubes tied and their fertility eliminated. The truth is that we no longer need marriage to have children or to be parents. A child can conceivably have five different parents: a sperm donor, an egg donor, a birth mother, and the father and mother who actually raise the child. We will continue to reproduce whether we are married or not, whether we are hetero- or homo- or bi-sexual. No matter what, we are going to reproduce and make babies — it is instinctual to human survival, and the truth is we no longer need marriage to be parents.

Average life expectancy has risen dramatically in the last hundred years, from 30 to 40 at the beginning of the twentieth century to 75 to 80 in the developed countries in the year 2000. According to these statistics the average married couple will live for more than thirty years after the children leave home. No previous generations have been confronted with such a long-term commitment. We have surpassed all previous life expectancies, and are living to an average age of 78 in the United States. When one can expect to have at least three careers in a life time, what happens to the idea of one marriage to one person until death do us part? Are we suggesting unreasonable lifetime commitments? In the evolving paradigm, our lifestyles, careers, and even love interests shift in a changing world.

There is no need to challenge the validity of traditional marriage, but rather to examine and move forward toward integrating new marital and familial paradigms, while respecting what has been established, and allow for the voice of the Other to be part of the conversation. This voice relieves the pain and suffering of humanity by acknowledging the emergence and evolution of human consciousness. Everything on earth that lives and breathes is our child. And everything that sustains us is our Mother. Every son and daughter is our baby. Each of us has a divine purpose and service on this planet. We are living in times where we are all responsible for breaking down the barriers and treating each other as family, not only by the confines of our stocks and bonds, but by our devotion to the sacral nature. We are the new paradigm.

Courtly love in the Middle Ages can be seen as an origin of the modern notion of the personal self, the cultivation of personal ethics, as contrasted with conformity to a religious doctrine. Early Renaissance romance portrays life in terms of a personal quest. The individual leaves the security of the family, overstepping boundaries, and voyages into the unknown. The quest for love is a private rather than a public matter. Romantic love is a portal for transcendent experience, both erotic and sacred.

By the eighteenth century the spirit of revolution spread from America to France and eventually to the rest of Europe, as people threw off the bonds of monarchy and embraced the ideals of "liberty, equality, and fraternity." These democratic ideals gradually began to transform traditional marriage structures. Women sought equality in education and voting rights, in the workplace and on the homefront. More and more wives, who were previously little better than indentured servants, became industrious, thrifty workmates and companions with rights of their own. Living in a "free society" fostered greater freedom for men and women to seek mates based on attraction and affection, cutting across ethnic, economic, religious, and racial barriers.

In our current world, erotic passion and romantic bonding lead to marital love. Intimacy and dialogue secure the attachment. Marital love has become more fully sexualized, romantic and intimate, fueling intellect, enjoyment, and soul enlightenment.

The choice for the romantic and passionate experience transcends established boundaries and the security of the known and leads into the terrain of the unknown. Romantic love voyages into the realm of erotic desire and phenomenal experiences that open into the transcendent dimensions of the sacred, returning us to traditions of love and marriage that are compatible with our human spirit. This is the romantic ideal.

When courtly love first blossomed, marriages were familial business arrangements, devoid of passion, and the outlet for expression, depth, and romance was outside of marriage, between "the man and the lady." Devotion was between lovers. They formed bonds free from social conventions. Mixing romance with marriage transfigured the concept of marriage, and by the twentieth century there was a complete reversal — now the adventure of erotic passion is the prerequisite for marital union among most couples.

Marriage and love merge. Courtship takes on a new meaning: marriage in the name of love. Romance is a world of spontaneous feelings, imagination, and divine inspiration that drives passion, seeking a container for the sacred erotic. Unbeknownst to young lovers, by the grace of the beloved, the quest is for none other than sacred love.

The Images of Love

Every one of us knows deep down that we are worthy of love, because love is in alignment with the heart and soul. How then do we develop our images for love and romance? Love images are conscious fantasies which parallel our dreams and desires. For those of us who experience nurturance and love, these encounters are catalysts for realizing our divine potential. For those who suffer early painful encounters with loved ones (parents, guardians, family members), their love images are ideals opposite to that painful experience, and attempt to compensate for the suffering and loss of love. Individuals who encounter early abandonment seek a secure attachment. For those who grow up in a family by which they feel imprisoned, dreams of being rescued ensue. Those whose families are cold and detached orient towards a partner with a warm and loving tribe. All of us, no matter what the situation, are striving towards wholeness, attempting to complete what is incomplete, to bring about the restoration of love. For many their life path is the spiritual search for love.

The many encounters on the path of love integrate, and one becomes the image of one's own divine ideal. There is no longer an external expectation for the lover to fulfill the imaginings. Individuals who are firm in their sense of self are no longer threatened by differences or personal preferences. They are expansive enough to engage in dialogue and negotiations. In these relationships, couples appreciate their separateness, experiencing their individualism as well as their union. They are compatible and complement one another's goals and desires. Romantic love cultivates interdependence, experienced as the interchange between love and freedom, union and autonomy. "Human love promises to initiate us into divine love." The intention of love is to awaken to the Beloved within our hearts. We realize the internal purpose of love and its connection with all of life. The beloved is "a window onto the divine." As the soul matures and refines, one begins to experience self-actualization, transcendence, and a taste for divine love.

Romance

Romance originates in a deep desire to know yourself, and is found in engagement with your own soul reflected in the beauty of the environment. The ideals of the "romantic" are deeper desires to love yourself in a way that no other has ever loved you. It is dressing sexy, massaging head to toe, wearing your best scents, dancing and singing while doing your chores. It is eating colorful, sensational food. It is bubble baths and candles, drinking the best wine. It is touching your body, discovering your erotic hunger, your orgasmic nature. It is as if you are he or she, and he or she is there. The Beloved is silk and takes you to ecstatic bliss. Constancy and devotion to personal love cultivates self-respect and admiration. When we identify what it is for ourselves then we are identifiable to those who are capable of meeting us in this erotic dimension.

Romance actively revolutionizes our consciousness. It draws forth the imagination, our ability to play, and stimulates our emotions. Romance directs the love experience. If romance is absent, a dimension of the psyche is cut off from expansive love. Love can happen without romance, but in time it falls short. Without the romantic dimension, boredom quickly ensues. Structure and routine are hard to bear. Romance keeps everything moving and flowing.

When courtship is the foundation, love is strong. Romancing between couples infiltrates the world around you. Love fosters more love and extends itself into all our relations. To fall in love with the world is divine appreciation. The love appears in everything, in the beauty of a dialogue with glory — in butterflies, birdsong, hummingbirds, in the sound and smell of desert grass, the call of a coyote.

Romantics at their best will tell you that life is great! Like springtime, ever new, they feel the life current teeming in their system, which gives rise to energy, enthusiasm, and meaning in life. When we are loved and loving, there is an attitude of joy and success which magnetizes abundance in our lives. Our income increases. Our awareness of what is important to us magnifies.

The shadow side of romance is raw, instinctual, lust driven, and strictly sexual. One feels exhausted, depleted, and drained by the "romantic" encounter. The partner is taking energy rather than enhancing your life energy. The bank account goes down, your work performance falters. If this is the case, you are not in a true romantic experience. You are with a vampire-like lover who drains your life and regenerates himself from your energy. The romance fades.

Home is where the Heart is

Our past experience draws us to constructs that are "just like home" — a needy person, "just like mom," or a dominant and overbearing individual "just like dad," a put-down teasing type "just like big brother." Our early wiring knows how to navigate these familial environments. We find ourselves in love with what was and is familiar. It is what we know. We are in love with the scent, the sound, the lifestyle and status, of another who activates the memory of home.

At first these memories are comforting, but in time they become very confronting. It's all light until it turns dark. Pain surfaces. We leave home to find ourselves, to separate and individuate. The journey is an endeavor into the dark which pulls us forward by the hope of illumination.

We strive, and discover that home is as near as our heartbeat. We are in the vicinity of home when our heart is expressing congruency between our inner and outer worlds. The heart resonates with love for self, others, and the world. The heart becomes a divine altar, a synergistic space which holds the past and present, who we were and who we are, and most importantly who we long to be. That which is longed for is courted. Home is where the heart is. We seek the friend who gives voice to our inner secrets, encouraging us to continue the journey. The same desire exists in those who have sought us out. Two streams exist in the harmony of one ocean, an ocean of love that brings it all home, not the literal experience of childhood, but the real experience of a magical kingdom where the mystery of Self, purpose, and destiny unfolds.

Love and Security

Is romantic love a brief prelude to stable love? Popular belief suggests that once reality intervenes and one gets to know the other as he or she "really" is, the idealization that fuels the illusions of romantic love are no longer possible. Many consider romantic love a dangerous and unstable basis for shaping a life. This produces the belief that romance and stability cannot co-exist in a steady relationship. We often hear the example, "I love you, but I am not in love with you." To "be in love" re-asserts the realm of passion and fantasy. The psychological transition to "I love you" creates a stable and sober reality. The conviction of a "steady, firm relationship" is in conflict with the innate desire to be "in love."

Yet clearly the nature of relationship, indeed of reality itself, is fluidic and ever-changing, even in the context of the marriage container. We create the illusion of stability and security and attempt to satisfy needs that are constantly changing and redefining themselves. One moment a person is completely content and in the next minute restless, insatiable, and desirous for something different. For some, marriage restrains individual freedom and the right to exist solely as a contributing individual. For others, individual freedom is a lonely burden, life is difficult to manage, and they seek the confines of a marriage container to cope with overwhelming responsibilities. Both love ideals are a state of mind which defines your own personal encounter.

For instance, wealth is a state of mind. Some people have millions of dollars yet are mentally forever poor. Others are just getting by with their finances and experience a very wealthy life. And so it is with personal freedom and inner security. When personal freedom and inner security are in alignment, one's picture is passionate and self-revealing. If, however, driven by external compliance, one's outer image clashes with one's inner definition, one is subject to function in a culturally created reality, and experiences ongoing conflict. In the midst of all our personal constructs, love itself is a constant presence which is translated into a felt experience. And this love is constantly evolving and deepening as our true expression.

When we are engaged with a love experience, growth, transformation, and synergy are part of the conversation. Depth and intimacy nurture Eros, a realm that supports interesting, desirable, and spontaneous outcomes. When we harness these energies, the psyche automatically feels like a captive to the structure. Eros replenishes and vivifies a creative, unpredictable flow, the perpetual flow of love.

Fixed external conditions make for unstable internal conditions which incapacitate life. The excitement of the unknown is diminished by the known and drab. Boredom, a type of psychic impotence, arises and gives way to exciting fantasies. Adventure seeking, boundary crossing, and repressed desires translate into virtual realities. Eros is interpreted as pathology when a person is driven to seek release in forbidden territory. Eros has no place for the stable, mature, and married. Consequently spouses are expected to console themselves by "sublimating" their desire into a "creative project." Furthermore, the psyche copes by identifying this action as a "choice." We are taught to tolerate, control, redirect, and even renounce our desires by continuously rededicating them to the bonds of matrimony.

Predictability rules the relationship. Habit and structure produce the illusion of security. Couples contract and form "collusive contrivances." For example, they talk themselves and each other into believing they could never have love and desire with anybody else. Why then are there so many extra-marital affairs? Not only are they common but they are emotionally shattering. In truth, neither party may be so sexless and so saintly. Partners collude to create states of security by predicting behavior and constructing patterns and habits. Habit kills desire and produces boredom, which is deadly to relationships. Habit is not intrinsic to love and defends against the more vulnerable experience of romantic love, which allows for revelation and discovery of the other.

People can bring with them unconscious agreements, cultural training, and repressed role models, which can cause them to say things like: "Oh, let's not upset the apple cart." "We don't want to go there." "We don't allow ourselves to feel passion or desire." "We just maintain to keep it steady." I am not saying that the steady, harmonious relationship must invite chaos in order to flourish. What I am saying is that these kinds of psychological boundaries infantilize the relationship and keep it in a certain state and stage and then… people encounter tragedy, death, catastrophe, change, and it is like a volcano. Everything that has been stewing, simmering, and burning explodes. All the stuff they never discussed or dealt with begins to have a life in the relationship, and it is completely overwhelming.

That is why Eros/romance and security/stability are in a dynamic tension. It is the way to keep the love alive. Otherwise love dies. It suffocates because there is no place for it to have expression in your life. There has to be a balance. You don't want to act out extremes, the place where neither one meets the other. Fighting and pecking away at one another is not healthy. We need to be open to spiritual and psychological growth. We as human beings cannot stop growing and cannot stop dying. We are growing and dying at exactly the same time. From the moment we are born until the day we die, we are dying. Every cell in the body is dying, and we are growing new cells all the time. That which dies off gives birth to life.

Developmental History

Couples who are overprotective of their children are called "helicopter parents." The parents' tendency is to screen out potentially harmful and dangerous situations. Children are protected from having to confront their own worries or fears, or even their personal creativity, spontaneity, and joy. The unknown is dangerous. When these children become adults, they have a strong motive to join with a partner who re-creates that same sense of security and has been shaped by similar parenting techniques.

A safe and secure environment is psychologically necessary for a child to form healthy bonds and attachments. Human infants, unlike all other species, need their parents in order to survive. We are biologically dependent on our parents for our survival. To develop and form a sense of self, we need stability, or else we find ourselves cracked up and fragmented. Stable, secure parenting reflects worth, importance, and builds self confidence. However, over-protection produces self-doubt. You don't trust yourself. Others always know what is best for you. It erodes self-confidence and the innate desire to take risks, to learn, and to grow. The challenge arrives when, in our adulthood, anything foreign or unknown is assumed to be dangerous. As adults we have no idea how to live beyond what we already know. A spiritual teacher once said, "Just because it is our experience doesn't mean it's correct. To learn and grow we need to move beyond our experience." We all need to be vulnerable to the risks that come with love.

Just reflect and be honest for a moment. Has there ever been a love that is secure? It is our nature to be curious, to be interested, to wonder, and to evolve innate attributes which produce great discoveries, inventions, and even new models for love. Disappointments and heartbreaks are unpredictable and painful. Yet despite our own wisdom, we still strive to make love secure. I don't know a person who actually grows who doesn't experience pain to accommodate growth. For a time pain is the companion of growth. With growth we experience loss and grief.

We all inherit family values and belief systems and collude to incorporate our partners into them. Then one day you wake up and find that the partner you attracted out of your inherited belief system doesn't fit with your true identity and sense of self. What you originally admired and trusted, making you feel safe and secure, has transformed into a suffocating, stifling, repulsive situation. The next thing you know you're having a love affair.

Affairs readily occur at any age and are more typical at mid-life. They are viewed as age denial, the opportunity to "reclaim the adolescence I never got to have," or to have an "extended adolescence." These feelings are especially true for people who marry young and establish their identity through their partner. Sex with someone outside the marriage is hot and passionate, unruly and risky. Just the sex by itself is a rebellious act that dissolves the marriage contract. Extremes give birth to extremes. When it surfaces it is powerful and has a life of its own, taking you beyond your comfort zone, even beyond your comprehension. This is a powerful time to revisit and redefine who you are in relation to who you thought you were, and recognize that you need to change. Courtship with the beloved is about stepping into your true nature, your divine nature and sacred inheritance. It is about becoming a "soul conscious" individual. Love takes a new form. Couples work to be conscious and agree to be expansive. Personal growth and evolution is a friend in harmony with personal pursuit.

Healing the Split and Remembering Our Connection

Let's consider our sameness with a partner. We have been culturally indoctrinated to believe that that which attracts us is our opposite. The truth is that our opposite is our sameness in a different form. The "attraction" is what is waiting to be actualized, or realized.

"A is an astrologer. W has dabbled in astrology and her profession is psychology. A is actualizing his astrologer. It appears different to W because she is actualizing her love for psychology. By expanding into A's perspective, W learns about planets and their archetypal influences. This is where A & W meet in their sameness — they both are intrigued with archetypal influences and their effect on an individual's psychology. Being in A's presence reveals a dimension and understanding which is more advanced than W had experienced prior to choosing him as her mate. As she grows in her sameness with him, he also grows with her, learning and exploring the benefits of psychology. Neither of them needs to become the other, yet by being together they experience their sameness in a different form."

A person doesn't have to have a motorcycle license in order to love riding on the back of a motor bike. Both the driver and the person who rides are in their "sameness." What makes them different is the level of actualization the person has reached with his/her attribute or interest. When we see someone as our opposite, the message is to oppose, and this splits us from our state of connection and wholeness. In the realm of courtship, recognizing our sameness is revealing and integrating to our wholeness. The expansive, creative flow between two people, the soul conscious connection, develops and reveals

83

ourselves to ourselves in and through the presence of each other. This is the gift of Eros. Mutual passion between two people mines the unknown, and brings our love into a state of consciousness which deepens our relationship to the Beloved. We can express the same thing with different words, even having different values and points of view which appear opposite.

Although it is our intention to experience a new and different love from our last, we often find ourselves in a matrix that recreates itself no matter whom or how we choose to love. The mystery behind this phenomenon has to do with the unconscious seeking to resolve a hurt or paralyzed place through love. The love that is exchanged in a healthy dynamic gives this place of paralysis attention and brings awareness to the pain seeking its resolution. It can feel like a curse which in time is revealed as a blessing. The key is to look at the place of repetition. When we tend to that place in the relationship, it moves the intimacy further along and brings a flow of love into the relationship. Damming up the love against the wound and ignoring the pain eventually erodes and breaks down the trust and intimacy. Despite our efforts, we find ourselves over and over again with a mother or father figure that our partner profiles, both the good and the ugly. It is the good that magnetizes and the ugly that is seeking its healing through gentle partnership and sometimes professionally skilled attention.

Obstacles to Intimacy

Sex is a vehicle for discovering one another outside the security and structure we create in everyday life. It is the place where we take off our clothes and are exposed at an entirely different level. Veils and cloaks drop. We are stimulated and enticed by the potential that arises through relinquishing control to a sweet surrender of self to the other and vice-versa. Through intimate bodily contact we arouse, entice, and tease. By our surrender to the sensations, we experience gratifying surprises when we open beyond our boundaries and allow ourselves to emerge and immerse in the sensations and rhythms of our love making with each other. Too often the sexual relationship is encumbered by immaturity, lack of sensitivity, power struggles, and limitations. Letting go into the experience means going beyond comfort zones and limitations to experience something greater. "Don't touch me there." "I don't like that." "That's gross." "I'm not going to do that." — these restrictions deaden Eros, lack surrender, and limit the enjoyment of love making. "Make love, not war" has its wisdom. If you're using your sex to fight your battles, you have some personal work to do. If you have hang-ups, shame, requirements, and restrictions, deal with them not in the bedroom with your lover but rather with the confidence of a trained professional.

Sex is a place where we can act out our wounds and express paralysis, because sex involves exposure. Some lovers are more intimate and comfortable in the bed than they are in the day-to-day life of a relationship. "As long as we don't leave the bed, everything is great." As the demand for interpersonal relating outside the bedroom increases, you may find your sex goes from bliss to agony in seconds flat. "Love is sex and life is hard." When someone doesn't feel love in their life, they can become dependent on extreme intimacy for self-assurance. It doesn't hold because in deep love making we lose definition and merge with the other. After the sex, the ego self returns and with it control, judgment, and criticism toward the partner. Everyday life requires an ego and this can override the incredible intimacy shared in bed. In general when these issues persist it can be due to a lack of maturity, experience, and personal woundedness. This is a sensitive issue and may require intervention. Don't take it out on your lover. When sacred sex remains dormant or unrealized, what is beautiful and cosmic becomes dark and plummeting.

Romantic Sex

Sexual trust develops and grows through satisfying and positive experiences. The love makers begin to touch realms of desire beyond their imagination and enter the realm of spiritual experience. Sexually romantic courtships are based on sexual participation and agreements. The "other" becomes more important. There is a heightened sense of desire which transcends and takes the love-makers into boundless, timeless territories that energetically affect the heavens. It is mindless and beyond the physicality of the body. You enter into a divine province. Intense sexual desire increases our vulnerability. It is best for the couple to gain rapport through the course of time, sexually courting one another out of respect for the dimensions they are growing into, agreeing to enter these realms that transport our fantasies. If one or the other exerts control, the risks can be detrimental, especially if they are insistent. This can happen when they are at their peak. So be careful. Take time, listen, learn, monitor yourself, and remain sensitive to the other person's needs. Notice if they are sensitive to yours.

I know of a situation where the minute the woman expressed her hunger to orgasm her male partner would withdraw, leaving her frustrated and dissatisfied. In her most heightened and erotic state, surrendered to his omnipotence and fulfillment, which made the sex incredibly high, he would diminish her because her erotic power sought orgasmic satisfaction. In a sacred scenario her orgasms would extend the love making and prolong the hunger. Over the course of time, it became his habit to hold the sexual power in the relationship. It was his decision when to have sex. In both the bed and the relationship he had no desire to fulfill her needs, only to have his needs fulfilled through her. What was once playful and enticing transformed into a narcissistic and sadistic game.

A significant difference with high sex is that there is a consistent attention to each other in the experience, which directs the love-makers to continue. This kind of high sex is subtle and deepens and evolves over time. In the context of two healthy and mature lovers, he prolongs the sex by allowing her to enter into orgasm, which multiplies in waves as he surfs in the ecstasy. Each time the lovers encounter a new experience, with no attachment to a specified outcome, allowing the erotic dimension to create itself through them.

Don't be surprised if a kind of amnesia around the details of your experience follows. This is often due to the transpersonal dimension to which you journey. It is best to allow it to be carried in the body. It is important to be conversant, check in, refrain from analyzing the encounter, and try to remain connected. Carry the bliss into the rest of your life and share the love in your relations and the world. A beneficent approach allows you to remain in the stream of divine consciousness.

When we practice the courtship of love as an art, spiritual devotion is present. Love making in and of itself is a prayer. Living love is the art. People who have a daily spiritual practice find over the course of time that they are met by a divine presence when they sit and pray. The energy grows and the connection deepens. It is as if your lover is waiting for you and instantly you go into a merge, which electrifies your cells and connects you to the Divine. There are no expectations. It is about showing up in deep surrender and allowing the Divine to take a hold, connecting the umbilical cords of your hearts. And when you finish the prayers, the connection carries into the day and all of your transactions. Your prayers benefit you by creating a deeper connection with the Divine and benefit those around you who, by knowing you, know love exists.

Sexual Fantasies

Fantasies dwell in the imagination of the person who experiences them. When what you want or desire is not what you're given or allowed, fantasies arise in the imagination to compensate for the unfulfilled desire. This sets up an automatic conflict between the internal and external worlds. Without constructive outlets (poetry, music, creative expression) or healthy sexual models, fantasies build and gain potency, which lead to extreme desire. It can feel dangerous to bring our fantasies to someone whom we are dependent on to maintain a sense of security and structure. This produces anxiety, which contributes to the inner conflict. Instead, fantasies are directed towards strangers or involve other people with whom we can act out what we were taught to repress early on in our lives. It is important to note that our fantasies inform us about our desires. It is the inner intuitive image for experiencing the mysterious which becomes displaced eroticism. The more one denies, the more perverse and potent the fantasy.

Central to every sexual position is connection, a connection we all long for and desire. It is our personal work to discover how we get turned on, which informs a deeper desire, that which we long for and has been denied.

We crave what we can't have, and once it is had and known, it doesn't have the same strength or dominion in our lives.

We have been told it is not appropriate to act out our sexual impulses with the people we love and respect. We are taught that sex is dangerous and threatens stability and security. Intimidated lovers have difficulty initiating sex with their partners out of fear of losing control of their own erotic fantasies. Spouses become desexualized, impairing desire in the marriage. So lovers seek the erotic outside the marriage vows. One misappropriates the fantasies toward someone "other" than their safe partner — an object one can detach from, who does what one wants, and with whom one can do whatever one desires in order to serve one's appetite. We find ourselves attracted to "bad boys" in order to experience our "bad girl," or we are desirous of sexually explicit lovers who provoke and permit our own desire to sexually exploit ourselves.

The key to deviant behavior is degradation of the other, to treat your sexual partner as an "object" rather than seeing them as a person. When one deviates from conscious sex and exerts one's own power, the sex becomes a script and nothing new can happen. Another concern is exerting control over the partner to keep them from changing. Change causes instability, which threatens the false state of security. Sex is acted out in a contained, routine script to ward off any unknown risks in order to sustain a certain structure. A controlling sexual partner gives little or no consideration to the others person's needs, desires, or preferences.

Clandestine sex liberates the mysterious, marginalized desire. You have found the object of your desires. The challenge of continuing on in this way is that as long as you disown your sexual inner world, your lovers are nothing more than objects. The cure is to heal the split and trust that Eros in relationship is a natural byproduct of love. Sexual courting allows us to open the doors to our fantasies and fulfill our desires with the partners we love. Love the virgin and the whore. We all need to experience something greater, to reveal the unknown, to discover boundless pleasure, in our love making. Courting the erotic, we enter the bedroom chamber, a secure, creative container to explore and discover our erotic nature. We give ourselves permission to experience our sexual nature without restriction. Rather than entering a downward spiral, we experience ascension into a greater expression which nourishes and expands the co-creative impulse.

Love and Desire are One in the Same

The popular belief is that love and desire are exclusive. They co-exist in us, yet in our relationships we don't believe that love and desire exist in harmony. In fact love and desire are one in the same. Love informs our desire and desire informs our acts of love. We have been taught by our culture, our families, and our friends that the people we love and who love us are obliged to secure us. They are an anchor. As impressionable humans we have been conditioned to secure love and in order to secure love, we have to anesthetize our desire. We have been taught that desire takes us out of what we already know into parts of ourselves that are unknown.

In actuality our experience of love is always changing, and in turn affecting us to be different in how and who we love. It is painful to restrict and reserve our love. It keeps us from experiencing a divine flow. Love is splendid, a myriad of experience needed to discover our wholeness. After all, the only thing we can count on is that love is ever-present, ever-changing, and transforming. It is part of our natural evolution to experience discontent in the development of our love history. Rather than being threatened or depressing ourselves against love, we can reorient, explore, and inquire. Desire points in the direction of the undiscovered. Discovery enhances, nurtures, and promotes Self-actualization. In a world that is rapidly evolving, how we love and relate needs to be honored and embraced.

Genuine passion is not split off from a longing for security and predictability, but is in a continual dialectical relationship with that longing. "In order for romantic involvements to remain vital and robust over time, it is crucial that the commitment not be so rigid as to override spontaneity, and that spontaneity not be so compelling as to preclude commitment."

Imagining Realities Together

Courtship teaches us that the beauty we experience is in actuality the divine ideal which connects rather than separates us from the rest of the world. If love separates it is not love. Love unifies.

An altruistic model of relationship involves service to the self while in service to others. Altruistic couples operate through the generosity of their spirit, which is sanctified by their practice and connection with the Divine. Through this practice there is an evolution in the relationship out of which the extraordinary becomes ordinary — a life of synchronicities, serendipities, success, abundance, prosperity, and connection. The couple holds the intention of their ideal manifesting and realizes that the dream they are dreaming is dreaming them. The dream becomes a waking reality. When the extraordinary becomes more and more ordinary, we see the world through a window of transcendence.

Here is an example: We are envisioning a beautiful mansion. What are we going to do with a beautiful mansion? We could have rooms for our families and a special room for spiritual teachers. The central room could hold a circle of dancers, the salon could host astrologers, the offices will serve our patients, and in the swimming pool there will be joy and laughter. Now that we have found our beautiful mansion, what are we going to do with it? Who is living in this beautiful mansion? Two lovers on a spiritual path, family and friends, the privileged presence of great spiritual teachers, dancers praying for peace in the world, astrologers connecting cosmology with humanity, clients receiving services — and joy and laughter in the swimming pool. This is God's house, given to us by God, to house God's friends. We agreed on this ideal, this blueprint, long before we found our house. What was once considered a wish-fulfilling fantasy, imagined in a dream world, is life in vibrant fashion, with all of our relations uniting in love.

Imagination activates our emotions, which then shape and construct a world for ourselves that is quite real. It is when we deny the images and the voices of our imaginings that we find ourselves in states of disillusionment.

There is no magic. Living out our ideal, we come to realize that it all flows from our lips to God's ears and from God's lips to our ears. When we listen, we experience the divine as a living reality. We have been taught to believe that risks and acts of faith are disruptive and break down our world. In truth we are always deconstructing and reconstructing because it is the ontology of the soul to grow.

Authenticity, creativity, spontaneity, and sensuality are all conducive to the erotic relationship. In a mature adult relationship, romance and desire are essential to the health of the relationship, unlike our models from the near past. A belief was held that passion is the id gone wild. Permission was given to romance only in the beginning of the relationship, and then this beast was put in a cage so they could get on with their lives. Both partners colluded to extinguish the light that sparked the love to begin with. It is important to kindle rather than suffocate the fire. Heat is needed to assist two people to burn through into something new, redefining and evolving the love relationship. This is the art of courtship. We are all learning how to do it together. The intention for a shift in how we view love is essential. It is time to stop treating love and passion as a pathology and begin actualizing love in its original form.

There is often a deeper sensitivity, a kind of transparency that exists between two people who maintain passion and love in their relationship. Even in the most mature circumstances, the deeper the love, the greater the vulnerability and intimacy. There lives a delicate space between the place of everyday life and the pursuit of love and happiness. Our childhood is a precursor for understanding these matters. The psyche instinctually anticipates a correlation between passion and fear, depth and intimacy, which fosters dependency. Romantic longing and desire have no fixed or solid ground and can produce feelings of humility, arousing aggressive states and even dependency. Aggression is an indication of desire. It is important to remain aware that this level of delicacy, even fragility, involves a certain amount of risk and takes time to kindle until it turns into a burning flame. Sustaining romance requires a certain amount of balance and tolerance for the depths of our passion.

Romantic love is a process, not a set system, not love by the numbers. For couples to consciously enter into alternative love, they must be willing to deviate from their secure and familiar and to engage in spontaneity. The process involves an ongoing conversation, a dialogue that includes the exchange of desire and longing, not as a threat but as an invitation to expansion and growth.

For example, the beloved expresses a desire for world travel, to pack up the house and put all the possessions and responsibilities in storage, and journey with her lover into the unknown. The beloved imagines the journey as the destination. The lover has finally settled into the peace and tranquility of a predictable routine, and the idea threatens the tidy world they have made. The beloved reminds the lover that they are here together for a short while and the call to discover is present in this beautiful space they have created. The lover pauses, then returns to the dialogue, and also hears the heart call to the wild, the unknown, and feels the anticipating pulse of soul.

Romantic cultivation and commitment in relationship is about two people coming together in their individualism and their togetherness to generate a life that gives birth to love. It is the continuous conversation of hopes, dreams, and desires, their prayers for manifesting their fantasies as a reality. Their alliance is a process of personal challenges and confrontations, action and change. Both parties have to be in agreement to tolerate their differences and rise above popular cultural beliefs. More often than not, realities become fantasy and fantasies become reality.

Romancing the World

Courtship extends into the depth of ourselves and the world. A depth approach to romancing the world begins with conscious soul-tending through observation and knowledge of the heart. We tend to the chambers of the heart by confronting, cleansing, clearing, purifying, and discovering that our soul is love. Love is the essence of soul consciousness, a love consciousness.

Just try going out into the world where there is a group holding a strong intention for peace. Attend a class with the Cabbalists steeped in ancient mystery scripture. Sit with a Buddhist group holding the intention of liberation from pain and suffering. Spend some time with the Sufi mystics, who nourish their connection through divine remembrance and ecstatic dance. Hang out with the Native Americans, indigenous people who pray for the earth and the four-legged, with the women who are resurrecting the Goddess from the Christian graveyard, with the Hindu devotees who chant prayers from the heart, with the religious who pray the rosary daily, and with the recyclers who regard our natural resources. They are the spiritual teachers. This is the avant garde. There are millions enacting "Thy Light in all forms, Thy Love in all beings." They constellate a cosmic matrix woven together by *Ishk*, which is Arabic for love, the bonding agent, the universal glue that holds us all together.

These lovers and beloveds are soul-consciousness actively meditating, secret servants and temple tenders lighting candles at your next door. They are the individuals who dare to romance the world, and in so doing cast the "spell of the sensuous." They hold a beneficent intention that affects and creates peace, liberation, divine connection, and love in the world. Every soulful act is accomplished by love. By romancing the world, we are actively individuating to a love that stretches beyond the rules of our culture and family approval. This love exists beyond our past and even our present. This love spans into the future and actively affects the present. Now is the time to actively participate in creating love. Every gesture, act, walk, talk that is connected to the divine animates soul in the world. That which revolves in its turn evolves us from a social to a spiritual to a planetary culture. We are soul making, *animae mundi colendae gratia*, for the sake of tending the soul of the world.

I once had a spiritual teacher pose a question to a group of us. He asked, "Who makes love when we do?" This question immediately provokes a state of receptivity accompanied by a conscious awareness of how we perceive and witness the act of our creating. Body, heart, and mind are informed by our spirit, which directs the soul in its creating. We expand ourselves beyond our individual sense of self to incorporate the universe and discover that not only are we the weavers, we are the thread that is weaving.

Individuality as Love

Every one of us is a unique manifestation of soul. It is through our observation, creativity, receptivity, and intuition that we participate in soul practice, which in turn perceives and enlivens the Soul of the World. A world consisting of soul and spirit is a comprehensible reality. Engagement with this practice realizes our spiritual destiny. We are the microcosm of the macrocosm. Our inner and outer worlds converge and assemble as a space of deep knowing and connection. Our everyday reality morphs into a soul reality. As you open and create you are also being created as a soul-filled world.

Perhaps we are living with a question or desire. Soul is seeking connection. We listen and know our inner guidance comes in many guises. Curiously we experience a gleaming, even an unexpected visitation, revealing the answer to our question, which spontaneously meets another soul who too is seeking connection and revelation in the field of knowing, which continues forward, exponentially growing into a global experience.

For instance, I am soul seeking. A little lost ferret enters my field. I enter my neighbor's field, looking for the ferret's owner. I meet my neighbor and we enter into a spiritual field, which takes us into the community field, which connects us with the global field. The answer to my question presents itself as a ferret that connects me with my neighborhood, which directs me to a neighbor who is seeking an answer to a question. This brings us to a spiritual gathering that is connected on a global level.

The interior presence of love is the conscious incarnation of soul embodied. This manifests as radiance that translates as a world of beauty, promoting feelings of profound love and connection. The soul of the world is conscious in us.

Thresholds: The Birthing Process of the Individual

For many, we do what we are told and are told what is expected of us. Then in our development we come to a juncture, a crossroads in our journey, and we are met by intense turmoil. Inner turmoil necessitates deep release of whatever and whoever we think we are, a deep surrender. Space is made for creativity, ideas, and actions, and by our action we discover our sense of purpose.

For example, a person hits a dead end. One day the boss comes in to work and announces that everyone is going on furlough. The person begins soul searching. "What am I going to do? What is the purpose of my life? What do I really want out of life? What matters to me?" After the process of release and deep surrender, a week, maybe months later, a far-away voice answers: "Don't you love children?" She hears the voice of inspiration and says, "Yes! I always wanted to volunteer for Big Brothers, Big Sisters," an agency that provides adult companions for underprivileged children. There are no jobs, nor is she qualified, so she follows her impulse by serving as a volunteer. She loves working with children but feels she could make a greater impact if she were a social worker. So she goes back to school to become a social worker. As a social worker she is qualified to be hired by the agency and is so effective in her work that she is sought out to apply for executive director. She becomes the executive director and generates more income in the first six months there than anyone else in the history of the agency. Services expand to meet the needs of the entire state. Love is the mid-wife that birthed the person from a factory-line mechanic to an individual. She was committed to the process of soul searching, deep listening, attending to the creative fantasies of her imagination, caring for the longing in her heart, and gaining the courage to take an action. Extricating from the wounds and struggles of our past, we work to reclaim and maintain responsibility for fulfilling our own needs. Our love relationship deepens and holds in union with autonomy and freedom, with love and commitment, with interdependence, forming a compassionate model for love.

Compassion starts with the individual. To approach life with compassion loosens the grip of judgment and criticism of situations and events that are out of our control. Faith is the driving force behind compassion. Those who see through the eyes of compassion connect "the earthly with the universal spirit." They recognize the activity of the spiritual in the literal occurrences of everyday life. Faith joined with intent generates love in the world. To begin each day with compassion is an expansive view point which transforms the inner world into an outer world vision. I can't think of a greater gift that we can give to love than the refinement of our own individual soul. Know that you are one facet of a brilliant diamond heart and your work is to polish into your brilliance. Brilliance implies luminosity, a Self who is an individual, complete and whole, beyond the scope of the personal. Individuals are attracted to other Individuals. They are not a burden, they are a life enhancement. It is a relief to lovers and beloveds. It is the new model for success in love.

Individuals engaged in a soul-making courtship experience love as a creative force. Time collapses. They feel nurtured and energized. Their souls expand. It is the momentum which supports the purpose and meaning of our lives, our destiny, and our connection with love. It is a sensing into the unknown knowing itself in relation to you, recognizing that there is something more that wants to be made, in service to a greater mystery. The soul senses its own creation as "the recollection of the whole of creation."

Soul-making relationships deepen into a greater intimacy, and serve as a vehicle for creating and circulating love in the world. The lover and beloved experience the "other" as Beloved and Lover originating in the One Love. Love flows out from the cosmos, continuously renewing the energy field of the relationship. Soul-makers live in the questions: "What is the source of this love? Who is the maker of this love? What is the work of relationship? What is our purpose?" Courtship allows the opportunity for the soul purpose to reveal itself and awaken into the world sphere.

Soul-making threads the web, yielding an inter-connected arrangement, converging with "inter-relational consciousness," extending to friends and community. Soul-makers give birth to the reproduction of a soul consciousness, invisible forms of possibilities. Intentional personal action includes the collective. Meditation, prayer, and attention to the inner world sphere give way to soul development. Love awakens the source in all beings, animating as the soul of the world. Love expresses unity and communion with the Beloved.

Trends and Models

The "marriage revolution" speaks to married couples and the spiritually wed who are using their procreative energies to serve in the world. Here are several examples of soul-making relationships:

He is an inventor who specializes in open source hardware design and micro controller programming, and she is an event producer who creates events to remedy problems she sees in the world. She is a life coach and he is a wildlife preserver. She is a spiritual teacher and he is committed to sustainable living. He is an ecological activist and she supports animal rights. He works for health care and she is a biologist. He is a scientist and she is a medical doctor. He is a nurse and she is an emergency medical technician. They have different functions but a common vocation. They hold loving care for our planet and attend to humankind. They are birthing and co-creating a world of social, political, spiritual, and moral responsibility.

Sacred Marriage: Hieros Gamos

The spirit of courtship is the intention to join in sacred marriage. Courtship, the found art, is a lineage of lovers and beloveds who approach relationship for the pursuit of spiritual love. The true union is for those who recognize that their bond is sacred. Courtship is the ancient ritual enactment between god as lover and goddess as beloved, of embodied deities in human form. "I" consciousness "perfected carries the attributes of both sexes." Their harmonization expresses as the oneness of their sameness. The lover and the beloved balance each other. Each holds his or her own magnetism, which draws out a chemistry of exchange between two people. Their energies balance one another and awaken the love nature. The magnetic pull of one to the other and the affinity of their energies hold each other in the gravitational course of rotation which penetrates the entire universe.

The heart is a fertile field. Affection and permission are the seeds that bear entrance to eternity. Harmony is the result of two people using their union as a container to encourage, support, and express their individual potential. Obstacles indicate frustration due to a lack of expression, and produce disharmony. Harmony is a natural state. In a sacred marriage the awareness living in the relationship is that each soul is seeking wholeness, self discovery, and a sense of completion. Completion may be interpreted as gaining life experience and actualizing the potential of the "I," which aspires to its fullest expression as an embodied soul.

Sacred sexuality is the place where spirit materializes and manifests itself in form. Spirit is endowed in every human being for the purpose of manifesting. The lover and beloved imbued with spirit create and reproduce the sacred in their chamber. The procreative pulse gives birth and life to spirit. Making love is the expression of the passion of union and gives birth to beauty. By spiritual conception, a "third" is created and "a ray of light finds its place of incarnation," reproducing the Holy Spirit.

The beloved…is sensitive and touchy, arrogant and insulting, changeable and hidden. The beloved is free-spirited, full of surprise and life, playful, joyful, and enticing. The lover's attention is a constant source of attraction to the beloved. The lover softens in the presence of the beloved.

The lover is by nature a spiritually conscious human being. Lovers are sensitive and responsive to all. Once a lover commits himself to the beloved, he lays himself open to both the bliss and agony of that love. The lover sees the soul of the beloved, the attraction and the beauty. Lovers see souls. The lover's love is as sacred as his love to and for the Divine. There is no discrimination, because it is the divine manifestation of the One in human form. Courtly love acknowledges that, between the two, Love transcends and prevails as the eternal fabric of the cosmos.

Courtship

We can no longer depend on our relationship models of the past, our roles, classes, standards, traditions, and institutions, which are the culprits of the loss of love and the sacred. We are driven to reevaluate, out of the chaos arising, the ongoing pain and suffering, and the deep dissatisfaction in relationship. We live out the archetypal love stories of time immemorial, due to the reticence to change. In this new century we are called to be whole. It is a renaissance of expression. Couples have to be willing to confront the "relationship culture" of the past and go through the journey of descent in order to rise and arise into a new consciousness of relationship. To settle into the illusion of contentment and security undermines a higher principle. For a new relationship paradigm to emerge we have to be willing to invite discontent into the conversation. It is good to respect limitations, but it can also infantilize a couple who never really blossom into a full courtship. In the container of a true courtship, the couple goes through all kinds of encounters, developments, and personal awakenings.

"One of the reasons J. and I are successful in our experience is because we didn't stop working when we found our love. On the contrary, when we came into love everything needed to be revisited and revised. Whatever got in the way of the love, we agreed to work on it. Our consciousness evolves and in that evolution there is an awakening to Oneself and the restoration of wholeness. We make love and then go and pray to our love connection. Or after we pray, we bring that connection to the lovemaking."

To revolutionize our love in the twenty-first century and recover the lost art, there has to be a willingness to say, "This isn't comfortable for me. Look at this with me. Out of love for the relationship I am willing to take a deeper look at myself." It is that willingness that enables a relationship to survive and takes it into depth. That is the *Ishk*, the love glue, the courtship. Self development means we are committed towards developing Self.

Refrain from trade-offs — "At least I know he'll never cheat on me," "She puts her passion into other things," "He has this problem but he is so great at that." When we make excuses for our partners, it's a real disservice to them. Unconditional love and positive regard is a beautiful gift one brings. What I am talking about is complacency, allowing, enabling the person to be stuck... so you can stay stuck. Which is worse? Trading off impedes your progress, your movement through the different dimensions of the love experience. Instead you are stuck in recycling the same old, same old things.

Spiritual nourishment can come from following a path, including the path of love. It is not unusual for one to find oneself increasing in magnetism and attracting people who may not be themselves practicing a formal path, yet are drawn to your shine. This can be both alluring and conflictual if the new partner has no interest in pursuing or participating with you in your spiritual resource. Often lovers will abandon the path, practice, even their place in a spiritual community, and transfer their energy to the new love interest who readily absorbs that energy and without reciprocity depletes the lover. These types of relationships are quick to dissolve. The key is to stay with the practice in the midst of the new love, and hold the intention to participate with a mate who is in resonance with a similar vibration of love and devotion.

Courtly love is dedicated to sacred love, a true monogamy centered on the One Divinity in humanity. Focus and concentration harmonize purpose and intention. To bring honor to the courtship one must approach it with loyalty. This is the path of awakening the heart to love. This resonates with the soul, and from it the soul gains truth and wisdom. Long, seek, find, develop, mature, and devote. Prayers and desires organize themselves under the conspiracy of the stars. Suddenly everything and everyone connected to your desire and longing manifests as love. Spiritual marriage is the intentional purpose to serve soul in service to the life that has been given. Lovers who are aligned with a common interest advance in life together and "stimulate each partner to progress on the path." Their vision is centered on the same goal. Love is light, the current giving life to the sacred. Love forms a trinity of energy between love, lover, and beloved.

Many fear losing themselves to love. The truth is you find yourself through love. You discover that you are love itself. Love is the expediter of Self-realization, the allegiance to the Beloved. Nothing can tempt nor touch it, nor break it down. Sincere love permeates relations in the world. The lover is in-spirited, and enters a sacred trust by this divine communion.

Withholding love or dividing love interests breaks down the power and influence of an intention. The energies are diffused and scattered, and in turn produce painful results for all parties involved. Lovers must purify to strengthen the heart. To be sincere toward another reserves the heart for no other. For the broken-hearted there is collective mistrust toward love. For the lovers, a true courtship is the opportunity to regain that trust. "For the joy and devotion to the One alone with joy and loyalty can only be known to the devout on the path of love." When lovers meet it is a divine re-union. As one of my spiritual teachers once said, "The thing about friends is that we find each other from lifetime to lifetime."

Chapter Seven
Love and the Erotic Pulse

The inner secret is identity with the Absolute. There is no separation. She/he and the Beloved are One. That which she/he has been searching for builds as a strong magnetism drawing forth each to the Other, deepening in the mystery of soul and deepening the Lover in the nature of God.

The human heart is the temple of transformation and the motivating force in humanity. Psyche and Eros activate the imagination. Sensual images, sensations, and thoughts produce arousal. This is the material of fantasies and dreams, the soul's desire. The body communicates in erotic terms. The onset of erotic content affects our emotional stability. The lover is potential, that which fulfills our fantasies. Flows of images generate the body pulse. Blood is stoked, giving way to sexual energy.

Psyche seeks communion between body and spirit. The erotic pulse seeks the sensual. We journey into the depths of our souls and the chaos of the heart, provoking repressed emotional states. All the associations and the "stuff" of love surfaces. The journey begins. It is messy and mysterious. The meltdown of the heart is a fragile undertaking of great suffering — the confrontation of the remote memories of our past with the desires for our future. To remain in close contact with the unconscious material and unpack its meaning is an arduous task. Tilling the ground for a fertile soil brings renewal and a shift in consciousness. The flesh is a sacred vessel, possessing the inherent drive to reveal the soul of our matter.

Uniting our consciousness with our erotic nature is a catalyst for actualization. Exploration of unconscious material directs us toward psychological health. The hidden treasure residing in the structure of the psyche guides us toward and through the love experience. Eros binds and acts cohesively, forging a connection between the self and the longed-for reflected in the divine. The Source loves its creations, and the created longs for its origins. Lust is a natural instinct which, when delayed and courted, can mature as a spiritual awakening to creation. "The field of desire is one in which these differing vectors of the soul engage, rub up against one another, collide, mesh, melt, vaporize, coagulate, differentiate, and articulate themselves in forms, patterns, dramas, and stories, finding direction, and perhaps dissolving again, in a cycle of the soul's transformative experience."

The body is a micro-image of the macro-image of the cosmos. There is a relationship between the internal workings of the human body and the celestial realities. The composition of the stars resides in the chemistry of the human body, and transmutation occurs in harmony with planetary influences. Cosmic chemicals are the ingredients of love.

Heaven with the stars and planets and all of the constellations, as with the Earth, is made up of the five elements (earth, water, fire, air, and ether) which combine with the three alchemical principles (*salt, sulphur,* and *mercury:* body, soul, and spirit) to form the constitution of the human being. As the inhabitants of Earth, we are affected by the changes and transformative influences of the planets. At the time of our personal birth the cosmos is arranged in a unique astrological pattern, referred to by astrologers as the natal horoscope or star map. The archetypal influences of the planets shape the Earth's precious metals, as well as those residing in the human body. Love is the cohesive force that binds it all together in the One. Originally we were one and dwelled together in the greatest of harmony.

Alchemical Marriage

In the context of courtly love, or the quest for divine love, the alchemical pursuit is a pathway by which two lovers utilize their relationship as an alchemical beaker for spiritual realization. Characteristically, the couple is inclined towards a psycho-spiritual marriage, each in conscious agreement and consensus to work through opposing egos and personal obstacles to love. They each take responsibility for the effect their chemistry has on the relationship, and diligently work away from separation and toward unification. The alchemical journey of Sol and Luna serves as a metaphor for the different levels and alchemical stages a couple undergoes to transform lead into gold.

Hermeneutics is the term for the formula according to which alchemy is happening in and to us, rather than being something outside us which we are observing. It is the interpretation of a subjective experience, the scripture of our interior text. We are the alchemical vessel, and our chemistry affects its operations.

Alchemists refer to *nigredo* and *solutio* as the lesser work and *coagulatio* and *rubedo* as the greater work or *magnum opus*. The *opus* is the spiritualization of the body. The lesser and greater cycles are psychologically experienced as death, rebirth, and resurrection. "Psychologically, we might say that consciousness grows through cycles of union and separation, through seeing the difference between ego and other and transcending that difference." This occurs repeatedly throughout the lesser and greater work. The false identities of the ego dissolve and evolve into a Self, one's true being and identity. Dying and dissolving is the *mortificatio*. The primal material and the examination of the personal shadow are confronted in the *nigredo*. This stage includes dissolution, putrefaction, and purification.

The alchemical journey between Sol and Luna is a story about the realization of love. Sol (Sun) and Luna (Moon) represent the archetypal masculine and feminine principles of our inner being. It is important to note that the traits of masculine and feminine are identified as Sol and Luna. The coupling in and of itself has nothing to do with gender. Same sex couples who are developed in masculine or feminine traits can seek completion through the other by the transference of opposite qualities. The alchemical courtship involves a series of stages. At each stage the union is refined and purified. Each operation brings the other closer to the embodiment of heaven here on earth.

Love is the cosmic chemical which summons each toward the other. They join as one. Coitus opens the matrix of their hearts as one melds into the other. Their fusion is a joining between opposites. Their lovemaking is lusty and motivated by passion.

The self is devoured by the loss of self-identity in the other. Deep and ecstatic lovemaking can simultaneously stimulate pain and trauma from the past. As each connects with the rage that reveals the impurities, the bind it holds is released and purified. The exchange of emotional intimacy is shared, each blending with the other internally. The co-mingling of masculine and feminine principles is felt as androgynous.

Fire and ash are followed by water, emotions, and tears, which release toxins from the system. In the process of purification and repeated cleansing the whitening becomes strong and clear, making our vessels solid containers for the accommodation of spiritual energies. The encounter in the dark *nigredo* and the purification of *solutio* prepare the alchemical vessels for *coagulatio.*

First they must separate, which supports each of them to individuate. As Sol descends, Luna ascends. As Sol ferments into the ground of his being, Luna is influenced by the cosmic forces of the heavens. Each becomes acquainted with his or her own power, discernment, intuitive insight, and fertile creativity. They experience illumination.

In order for the true nature of our being to be revealed, we are called to awaken, through love, by love, and in love. Awakening is a painful process which involves a shattering of the old and an emergence brought about by sudden and spontaneous bolts of awareness.

In illumination Sol wakes to his true Self. He becomes his own light. Heaven and Earth meet and must be nourished — and root him in the wholeness of life. Luna is absorbed by the heavens; electrification by the stars connects her to the divine. Sol and Luna unite and resurrect as a corporeal body which has been spiritualized.

Sol and Luna enter the final phase of *sublimatio*. As individuals now, their connection guides and nourishes them. As illuminated beings they hold in conscious awareness the immortality of life. Their hearts unfold as a rose, reddening (*rubedo*), multidimensional, and multiplying into a garden of endless fertility. They have caught a glimpse of what is to come, and again descend, die, and join as androgynes. As the sun and moon blend, she begins to become man and he begins to become woman. Two hearts fuse as one and in this erotic fusion rise towards the heavens. Their hearts are forged in royal gold, and now recognize each other as King and Queen. As their energy rises their bodies attain yet another resurrection. By their consummation, they are wed in a sacred marriage to God and become fully divine.

Confessions of a Serial Monogamist

"Love, for me, has been a spirogyra art. I have had many relationships in love, and as I reflect on my journey, it was as if all my encounters with love were occurring simultaneously. Love transcends time, each and every relationship was not a forever but an ever love. I realize that in each boyfriend, husband, partner, best friend, lover, companion, etc. there were divine qualities present — and when I found my spiritual love, he possessed all of them."

Chapter Eight
The Inner Turn:
The Eternal Courtship

The embodiment of love is nurtured by the continual remembrance of the Beloved. Invocations, prayer, meditation, and contemplation enhance illumination. Expressions of gratitude and praise strengthen the innermost nature of the lover, binding her to the heart and ever-presence of the Beloved.

Throughout the path of love there is a process of beginnings and endings. You may find yourself coming up short. For some mysterious reason your relationships just don't work. Your friends and family don't understand you. You're not like everybody else. They tell you, "You are so different. You are living on the fringe!" (One day I asked my friend, "What is the fringe?" She said, "The ornate decorations that hang from a beautiful cloth.")

There are also times when the ending of a relationship is actually a success. Your purpose has been fulfilled and the relationship self-completes. Relationships don't always end because two people fail; they also complete because two people succeed. There is still love between you, and love, as with other deep emotional layers, develops and transforms, beckoning you forward, expanding your capacity for intimacy and growth.

You might feel as if you are being propelled by an unseen force or power to move on. The more you fight against it, the deeper you suffer. It is a bittersweet encounter, which takes you into the depths of surrender, states of dark nothingness, with no past or future to hold on to. You may be alone for now, but not for long. Know that you have a new life in this death. Deaths are invitations to awaken.

Never-ending relationships take up space in the heart. One remains psychically mated in the debris of loves past. Grief is a process which brings the gift of conscious psychic clearing. Without grieving and completing there is no ending.

Endings are a time of deep reckoning. All the judgments you're holding toward yourself are obstacles to love. You are different now. Your heart longs for your forgiveness. Forgiving your past and your mistakes frees you from your limiting self and the other person. Forgiveness cleanses the heart and accommodates the soul to soar further, into the dimensions of the unknown. Forgiveness is attained when you experience release from pain and suffering, encounter self-acceptance, and experience peace. This is when your perfection begins.

Love matures and causes us to grow. It is not a linear process; rather it is a cyclical process. As we cycle through the seasons of love, we become mature in our loving capacity and gain a greater awareness for the path. We realize love is a journey, not a destination.

Up to this point you may have been "user friendly," subjecting yourself to relationships that deny your inner desire and personal standards. It is time to identify, clarify, and define what you want from love, rather than being whoever everyone else needs you to be. When you're open and boundless, you are more susceptible to experiences that define you rather than meet you as you truly are. Take yourself seriously, discover your value, and listen to your deepest dreams and desires. You not only begin to build trust with yourself, you also develop spiritual trust. Spiritual trust is attained by faith, which is trust in the absence of reason. Faith is the act of trusting our inner guidance, intuition, and inspirations.

Trust your own inclinations and perceptions. Refrain from depending on external opinions and judgments; they are nothing more than barriers on the path. Think about the confusion and disappointment you feel when you override your own intuitive nature. Trust your own perceptions. Faith is the bringer of joy and self-made success.

Spiritual trust is the acknowledgement that your thoughts and desires originate from the divine. The desire of the soul is a divine impulse. What you want is true. Spiritual trust develops by holding your intention which provides you with the strength, patience, faith, and determination to co-create and manifest your dreams and desires.

Be aware and discriminating. Too often we are eager to accept illusive visitations. This work can be tested by false promises and intoxicating appearances. Remain steadfast on your path. Alignment with the divine dissolves external dependencies and strengthens our inner sense of security. Know that love has an intention.

There comes a time on the path of love when the external world no longer satisfies our needs. Endless, senseless looking and seeking is accompanied by fear, anxiety, frustration, and disappointment. We find ourselves insatiable — nothing satisfies our need for very long. We come up empty, and loneliness is amplified. There is a constant longing and desire for something greater, which is difficult to describe or define.

This is the time for the inner turn. One turns within to discover, listen, learn, and evolve a spiritual passage into conscious relationship with the divine.

Spiritual Partner

Pain and suffering are the result of forgetting that we are spiritual beings. When we are not conscious that we are spiritual beings, we remain material beings, cut off from our spirit. "Spiritual attainment is making the spirit alive," and this is accomplished by becoming conscious.

Meditation is the practice of quieting the body and mind and allowing our spiritual nature to reveal itself in consciousness. Meditation evolves and awakens the heart. The focus is on the heart and the breath, often accompanied by spiritual mantras or sacred words. Sacred sounds are bridges to the inner world. Sacred words, in rhythm with the inhalation and exhalation of breath, activate spiritual qualities: intuition, inspiration, and heightened awareness. Meditation is a solitary pursuit, and yet you are never alone in the terrain of your soul.

Love has an intention. To discover love is to practice love. For the mystic, practice is private and personal. Through the various stages, the relationship with love itself develops and matures. One is courting love. Spiritual practice paired with depth psychological work brings forth self-knowledge. "The study of the self is really the study of God."

Let us now turn within. Close your eyes and focus on the heart. Set aside time every day. Create a space specifically for prayer, a place where you will not be disturbed. Awaken, cleanse, light a candle. Enter the chamber of love and sit with the presence of God. Allow images, thoughts, and reflections to visit. Breathe. As one goes deeper the silence penetrates, giving way to an illuminating presence. Inner guidance unfolds. Take counsel with, listen to, and speak to the whispers of your innermost being. In the union between your Self and God, lover and beloved, experience your communion. All the senses are heightened. Presence is palatable.

As the courtship progresses, one strengthens. One becomes more and more aware of one's true nature revealing itself in the intimacy of dialogue. Secure in your path with the Divine, anchored by an unwavering commitment, the real and true love is scripted on the heart. You are in the making. God is your spiritual partner. Dreams, desires, your precious prayers, are unique, essential to your nature, luminous, and imbued with grace. In the co-creative matrix of the divine, you are the eternal reflection of internal love. In this vibration you naturally magnetize people expressing a similar quiver. Human relationship is the outward practice of this love.

The inner turn is when we pull our energies away from the external to be with our internal world. When divine yearning emerges, we gather into ourselves and participate in the practice of divine remembrance. Meditation accommodates stillness of mind, peacefulness, a space to connect with essence, soul, and spirit. Dream the dream which is dreaming you, the dream that is dreaming itself through you into manifestation.

Depth Perspective

Awakening to love involves attending to metaphors, sensing, listening, and hearing. One is being present to presence by allowing the senses to be activated, while at the same time staying connected to the body. Metaphorical consciousness is in response to the call to remember our divine reality. Here is an example of how metaphorical consciousness is experienced in a depth psychological analysis.

"I am sitting with a patient, discussing her mother, with whom she has many issues. A spider comes into the room. Symbolically the spider represents the mother. The metaphor is the weaving of the web. The web is associated with feelings of having her life energy drained by her mother. The patient's impulse is to have me kill the spider. Questions are asked: 'Is killing the spider ethically responsible?' 'How is Spider informing the situation and exposing the belief systems of a pained individual?' Staying connected to the body through the senses, the patient now brings the mother's web into the conversation. Remaining with the tension of Spider in the room, the patient releases painful memories. I take the spider outside. The spider is liberated from the room, the patient liberated from the spider, as well as from the painful memories associated with her mother."

Sensing is the capacity to listen and hear in the present moment while staying connected and in the body. Projection separates the subject from the object. It is a way of avoiding responsibility. It is a way of being present and not really listening. A friend is telling a story, and you relentlessly interject your story into their telling. Sensing is letting go of attending to the ego. One is responsive and engaged with heightened sensitivity, allowing entry into the subjective field of another person. One is able to respond out of contact with presence. Soulfulness exists.

The interplay between sensing and presence evokes the "transcendent function." The realm of transcendence belongs neither to the conscious nor the unconscious. The transcendent function shows itself in making and creating beauty, expressed through each of us, as form with meaning.

Enter into a state of empathic communion. Allow silence to penetrate the space. Sense into the essence of the faculties informing you, bringing forth images, words, and ideas in the silence. Soul is making itself known. You enter a "style of being," deepening your consciousness, and participate in the mystique of the whole through relatedness. One enters the field of "psycho-logical" gnosis and experiences the intuitive apprehension of spiritual truth.

From the standpoint of "participation mystique," there is no separation of subject and object, of soul and world. Contemplate seeing the beauty in the world as the animation of the divine. The key to psychological gnosis is that soul matters; it involves recovering the body and all the senses. "We are in a field of flesh together. Mind cannot touch another's tears." Psychological gnosis is e-motional, knowing and being with what moves and touches us. Soul is present. There is no separation. Participatory consciousness is evidenced by meaningfully related events and synchronicities.

When we are actively engaged and participating in the mystique, we enter a dialogue of call and response. We admit to not-knowing, and this allows us to be who we are, to be open to the mystery of soul. We approach this with a religious sensibility — being open to the miracle which is opening us to a different kind of relationship with the world. The world dream is a place in which we are touched by the other, by the world — and the world is touched by us.

Dreams

Dreams are a portal to awakening. The dream is "the royal road to the unconscious." Dream tending is the practice of re-entering the dream, participating in the landscape of the dream in waking time. Dream interpretation occurs through the process of associations. These associations reveal images, themes, and figures from the unconscious that hold personal or collective meanings, and reveal in consciousness a place of wounding or a religious function of the psyche. "In the dream it is not only imagination and thought that work, but also intuition." The dream narrates something in the past or present — or something coming in the future, as in prophetic, visionary dreaming. Dreams can also manifest through the dreamer. The unconscious rises into consciousness in the form of a day-dream or imaginings during times of deep reverie. The dream is dreaming itself through you.

Here is an example:

"I remember it was summer time. I dreamed of the most beautiful pair of sandals. They were simple, brown leather, and cross-laced from the ankle to the knee. The next day I went for a walk in my neighborhood. I contemplated the dream. I didn't have much money, and I needed a pair of summer shoes. When I

was close to my house a sign on the sidewalk caught my eye. It read 'Free.' Beneath the sign was a pair of brown leather sandals with leather laces, just like in the dream! I picked them up and they were exactly my size! My soles (soul/s) were provided for by the great Divine!"

Here is another example, a waking dream:

"I was at a place in my life when my intuition was gaining momentum. I found myself knowing things with no apparent explanation. For example, I sensed that my financial consultant was misappropriating my funds. I wanted to take the For Sale sign off of my property. I had a concern that my home would be vandalized. I shared my angst with my friends, and despite my intuition I allowed them to convince me not to worry. Only later did I learn that indeed my financial consultant misappropriated funds and that my house was indeed vandalized within twenty-four hours of my gleaming.

"Shortly after these events occurred I found myself leaving work in the afternoon and coming home. I decided to rest, but had difficulty napping. I sensed something was happening. Again my intuition had kicked in, but I had no evidence. The home was very quiet. At a very precise moment during my reverie, I felt a little jolt. I got up from my bed and walked around my house, looking for what... I didn't know. Then I looked outside and sprawled on my deck was a glorious bobcat, a red lynx. I could hardly believe she was there, so I began taking photographs. She knew I was watching her, having made eye contact, and she began stretching, showing off her tail, yawning and exposing her canines, and then she sat down and faced me spot on. For some time we sat eye-to-eye as I contemplated her meaning and listened for her message. Solidly rooted in her power, Bobcat communicated to me the posture of majesty. I felt as if her penetrating vision could see straight through me. Her potency conveyed the wisdom of trusting my intuition."

Here is a prophetic dream:

"I had a dream that I was at an event. I was sitting among a lot of people. Everyone was wearing black and I thought I must be at a funeral. I woke the next morning and thought, 'My uncle died. I need to go to the store and buy a black suit.' As I entered the shower my wife said, 'What did you dream last night?' I was reluctant to answer and at that moment the phone rang. It was my cousin calling to tell me my uncle was dead."

Dreams are the terrain where inner worlds merge with the outer world. Dream tending allows us to identify significant moments which convey meaning in synchronization with phenomena in our waking reality. Dream journals and interpretations serve as a record of the inner dialogue and attend to the panorama of soul.

Deep Ecology

Life is a living prayer. Reverence for the earth and all of its inhabitants restores us to our spiritual nature. "By devotion, heaven is brought to earth." The unconscious is the consciousness of creation trying to make contact with us. Consciousness is more than exclusively human. Consciousness is collective. It exists in the plants, animals, stars, and trees. The "ecological soul" does not separate humans or anything else from the natural environment. It sees the world not as a collection of isolated objects, but as a network of phenomena that are fundamentally interconnected and interdependent. Deep ecology recognizes the intrinsic value of all living beings. We are connected to all of creation. Stars contain the same molecules and atoms found in the composition of the human body.

Human matter is elemental, made of earth, water, fire, air, and ether, the same constitution as our planet. The configurations that make up our bones also make up stones. The human heart circulates our blood, just as the rivers, streams, and brooks return water to the ocean. Our breath mirrors the whole of the world. Our metabolism is akin to fire. Our skin continually sheds and renews, as leaves fall from trees in autumn and grow back green in the spring.

Enter a forest. Feel the shift. Stand in the rain. Allow the dross to wash away. Lay on top of a mountain in the rays of the sun. Listen to the wind sing you a lullaby. Breathe the breath of God. Kneel and kiss the earth. There is a sense of deep devotion which arises by nurturing the deep ecology of soul. Love finds an outlet in the natural world, a bird, a flower, a ladybug, eliciting our awe, reverence, and worship.

The Ecology of the Soul

"As a child, I had an enormous weeping willow tree in my back yard. This tree was beautiful and strong, embracing and quiet. I would quietly sneak away to her for solitude and tranquility. When the wind blew, it would sweep and dance, and I with her. Time would pass. I took refuge in the soft grass that grew around her roots and anchored my body. I felt the sun stream through her branches, keeping me warm like a soft blanket. I would silently express myself to her in trust and knew that she was listening. I felt safe and loved in her sanctuary. My visits were ones of communion and contemplation. And as I developed, these attributes grew into reflection and Self-revelation. I would find myself in settings that would remind me of my willow tree, in spiritual environments, where people were praying, then where people were meditating, and then where people were speaking and teaching about the divine. Always I would relish the moment when I could sit under a tree, lay on a warm rock, sit in the ray of the sun, or reflect in the light of the moon and commune with that soft sacred place that introduced itself to me a long time ago under the weeping willow tree."

As the relationships between the two worlds develop spiritually, consciousness expands and is inclusive "in communion with all beings: plant, tree, mineral, animal, human and cosmic." The diversity of multiplicity exists in the unity of the One. Everything is connected by the essence of spirit. Reverence and worship for the natural world assists in identifying the sacred in humankind.

"One day I watched a homeless man dressed in rags standing at the entry way of a shopping mall parking lot. I parked my car and went over to hand him a dollar bill. He said, 'God bless you,' and his words soothed my soul. I went back to my car, where I sat and watched for nearly an hour as one person after another brought the man food, clothes, and dollar bills. He would humbly bow his head and say, 'God bless you.' I witnessed spiritual generosity pour forth from their hearts into his hands. The spirit of one man's soul was galvanizing perfection and divinity in the hearts of humanity. The joy I felt brought tears to my eyes and my eyes closer to the presence of the beloved interacting with lovers in the world."

The divine mystery seeks to reveal itself through you, through her, through him, by drawing forward what is hidden in our souls.

Chapter Nine
The Path of the Mystic

The lover evolves the courtship from the journey to God to a journey in God, a Union which has no end or destination, for it is taken in love as Love, and Love is infinite. The lover is awake and experiences the ecstasy of being and seeing that the entire creation is one with the Creator.

The mystical love poetry of Andalusia flowed into Provence and flowered in medieval courtly love. The art of courtship has its roots in mystical tradition. Mystical tradition is an oral transmission of sacred knowledge passed on from heart to heart, from generation to generation. Mysticism is symbolic and allegorical; it transcends the literal and encourages the transpersonal, inspiring a sense of mystery, awe, and fascination. Ancient mystery rites are endowed with esoteric practices to which only initiates are admitted. The basic premise of nearly every mystical path is that the initiate undergoes direct contact with the divine and experiences states of illumination. In the modern world mystical teachings are much more easily accessible, but actual realization is for most people only obtainable under the guidance of a spiritual teacher.

Mysticism is the pursuit of communion, identity, and conscious awareness of an ultimate reality, divinity, and spiritual truth. The comprehension of the Divine is attained through direct experience, fostered by sensing, personal insight, and self-knowledge. For the mystic, there is a deep intrinsic connection to the world and the experience of one's true blissful nature. What differentiates mystics is that they abide by no institution; rather they live as spiritual beings who are intuitive, open to the unknown, devoted to their faith and trust in the Divine.

Mysticism is an active expression present in the religions of the world and latent in the whole of humanity. The Christian mystic, Meister Eckhart said it this way: "Now the seed of God is in us. The seed of a pear tree grows into a pear tree. The seed of God grows into God." Rabbi Herschel suggests, "There is the grain of the prophet in the recesses of every human life." Buddhists teach that the seed of Buddhahood lies at the core of every sentient being, and its realization is the end point of our evolution. The Sufi mystic, Hazrat Inayat Kahn, states that the aspirant "... becomes conscious of one's own self in God, and of God in one's self ... deepening the consciousness of our innermost being."

Mysticism speaks to the innate will in the human soul to quest for the transcendent, to attain heightened awareness, and to maintain contact with the spiritual dimension which enhances life. The transcendent is ignited by a spiritual spark and lit by the fire of love. The invitation to love is the recognition that there is no separation. Everything is pervaded with presence which flows from a Divine Source. Everything we see is God. Everything we love is God.

The mystic is immersed in and responds to a mysterious life. They are the "seers" among us in the world. Loving sight is arrived at through committed practice and psychological work, transforming the "way" or manner of the mystic. The aspirant undergoes the complete remaking of character and the liberation of a new, or rather latent, form of consciousness, which imposes on the self the condition of ecstasy, a unitive state. Love awakens the heart, which is guided by affection and tender emotion. The heart is an intimate sanctuary, the gateway to the divine, the source of love and life energy.

The mystic is in love with the Absolute. The mystic presses at all costs and through all dangers towards union with the Beloved. The initiate is continuously being initiated into initiatory initiations. The journey from ego consciousness to Self-realization is intuitively perceived by the soul as cosmic or transcendental. With every descent into matter, the soul simultaneously and continuously ascends into spirit. The nature of the journey is one of circumambulation around the source, a sacred center, spiraling in between the outer and inner realities, gathering to oneself immanence in incarnation, the spiritualization of the corporeal opening into realization and the embodiment of the Divine. The mystic is the person who attains to this union.

The mystic path is quite natural to the seeker. There is an affinity with the teachings and practices, a type of "remembrance" in resonance with one's spiritual nature. The whole of one's soul is in alignment with the current of a particular stream. The path in and of itself is a total life transaction. Mystical revelation is personal and transcends limitations as one gains spiritual and self knowledge. One learns to understand life better. One's heart is always set upon the One, "the Beloved, the only Beloved there is."

The consummation of the path is love between lover and Beloved, expressing ever higher levels of reality, identification with the Infinite and one's eternal soul.

Spiritual Love

"Every relationship I have had has been religious, a kind of spiritual love, always in their successes and completions, always leading me back to the all pervading love — toward the One. "The Hindustani poet expresses it thus: 'It was the desire of finding an ideal love which brought me here upon earth; and this same desire of attaining the ideal is now taking me back whence I came.'"

"One sunny afternoon, nearly seven summers past, I was taking a walk in the bosque with my friend. We were chatting away about our desires, goals and aspirations. I was mindlessly going on about my heartache with love and wondering if I would ever find a man with whom I could be happy. In the midst of my chatter, suddenly I felt a rush of energy, maybe even some anxiety, stream through me. I felt as if my heart were cracking open, and I lost my breath.

"I panicked. I looked up into the vastness of the sky, and with the sun shining in my eyes I hit a deep silence. As I returned to my surrounding environment, I felt incredible joy overtake me body and soul. I exclaimed, 'Oh my God! The love I am seeking in a partner is the same love I have had with the Divine all my life! It has been God who is my perfect love, lover, and beloved, God who has served me unconditionally, who has guided me and provided for everything I have

ever needed, who has been present to me all throughout the challenges in my life. I am looking for a man to be my God-man.' I was instantly liberated."

Courtship with the Beloved

Courtship with the Beloved occurs when the inner life and the spiritual life merge. The inner turn converges with the mystical path. Tending soul articulates the deepening and re-collection of the eternal echo, the return of the lover to the beloved. The way of the mystic on the path of love teaches that "only the love of God can fulfill the desire of the human soul, and all other forms are only as steps that lead to the love of God. The love of God is living and everlasting and the love of the true Beloved."

The same principles apply to courtship with the Beloved in the spiritual realm that apply to courtship in a human relationship. Approach the courtship with devotion and commitment. Dedicate yourself to a spiritual practice and remain sensitive to daily nuances. Tune in through deep listening and refine the connection in contemplation. Love is reminiscent. As one becomes more and more absorbed, life is the instrument, the song of this love. As with your lover, throughout the day make contact, strengthening the bond and enhancing the courtship. Pray about your challenges and concerns. Convey your needs and ask for support. Witness the response in accordance with your thought. Recognize the spiritual demonstrations revealing and manifesting themselves.

"Late at night, in the pouring rain, I was driving an economy rental car in a rural area. It was so pitch black and rainy that I could barely tell whether or not I was driving in the right direction. I passed my turnoff and had to turn my car around. Turning around, I went off the pavement into a bog holding a week's worth of rain. My car wheels sank deep into the mud and after several attempts of spinning wheels I saw there was no way I could get the car out. The wheels were sunk in the muck of the earth. Time passed. I had no resources available. All I knew to do was pray and ask God for help. Out of nowhere this enormous truck stopped, flooding my car with its headlights. A bigger-than-life man got out

of this truck. Without a word, he chained my vehicle to his truck and pulled me out of the mud. I wanted to thank him, so I turned to get him some money. Before I could hand him a twenty, he was gone."

Even when you cry in the deep silence of the night, confess and whisper your secrets. Know that you are loved. In the light of every new day awaits a spiritual breakthrough.

"I was attending a school that required sixty hours of one-on-one supervision. The going rate for supervision was one hundred and twenty-five dollars an hour. I was student poor and had no idea where I was going to get the money to fulfill this requirement. I tossed and turned throughout the night, sad, ashamed, and embarrassed by my poverty. The next day I went for my morning walk around the neighborhood and was talking to God about my conundrum. At one point the wind blew up a gust and, as I looked up into the sky, a piece of paper came spiraling down. I reached for it in mid air. It was a check written for cash in the amount of one hundred and twenty-five dollars! I called the person listed on the check and she said, 'Oh, that is my mother! She resides in a nursing home in your area and has been writing checks and throwing them out her bedroom window.' I graciously agreed to dispose of the check. I knew that the resources I needed for my supervision were at hand."

In recognition of the Source, rejoice and celebrate. Give thanks to your Beloved in the same manner you would your lover — with anonymous love offerings, with senseless acts of beauty, with random acts of kindness. Tithing to the Source stimulates the universal law of reciprocity and the continuous flow of abundance and prosperity.

Dialogue with the Beloved

"One day my husband said to me, very carefully, 'I hear you talking away downstairs and I don't know who you're talking to…yourself, the cat, me?'

"I said, 'When I am not talking to you, myself, or the cat, you can know I am talking with God.'"

Spousal Mysticism

Courting the Beloved takes on new meaning when God is mystically experienced as Spouse, as "Other." Spousal mysticism is a direct way of experiencing God's love for us. During the medieval period in which courtly love arose, "spousal mysticism" emerged among the religious as a love relationship between the spiritual aspirant and God. These mystics approached the divine with a devotional attitude and commitment to embody spiritual tenets. Spousal mystics partake in a dialogic communion to access the depths. They are passionate toward their union with the Beloved. The lover enters the realm of the imaginal and shuttles between worlds, in and out of the mystical field of perception, the place of revelation in which the contemplative becomes aware of the Absolute.

Spousal mysticism is a process of being open to the influences of the "Other" through symbols, dreams, and images that hold personal meaning and expand individual consciousness. There is an intrigue and desire for the unknown, which encourages a receptive state for the unknown to make itself known through the seeker. The mystic attends to multiple perspectives by seeing through the eyes of the "Other" and listening to the unifying principles. The pursuit of "knowing thyself" is especially activated during personal trials and tribulations. The aspirant explores material he/she has marginalized or sanctioned to the unconscious and accesses information that assists with the deepest confrontations.

"I was out on a walk one day contemplating my value, worth, even my innocence. I was feeling as if something wanted to break through, a realization about myself that I could not identify. I was in a full blown dialogue with God, talking away as I struggled with my self-image. I remembered a time when I was a little girl and an uncle said to me, 'You know you are pretty... pretty ugly.' I felt a flush of anger come over my body and out of nowhere I heard a voice say, 'You are so beautiful.' At that precise moment a car stopped and the driver rolled down the window and said, 'You are precious!' and then drove on."

The unconscious is accessed by the process of contemplation, focusing on an idea or question, a thought, or a recent dream. Contemplation alters the state of consciousness and fosters the emergence of the deeper self as it enters into conscious life. The mystic crosses the boundaries of existence and passes over into that boundless life where subject and object, desirous and desired, are one.

Mysticism parallels experiences that facilitate contact with the deeper Self. The mystic attends to what is taking place on the fringes of consciousness. The lover is in possession of an instinct for the absolute, and is joined by the psyche, which directs us toward the meaning and purpose of our life. The deeper Self is the primary agent of mysticism, and lives a substantial life in touch with the "real" or transcendent world. Depth occurs whenever the personal experience goes beyond the control of the ego and brings us into a numinous encounter.

Spousal mysticism is the relationship between the individual soul, male or female, and the Divine. It is a spiritual marriage between the heavenly and the human. The aspirant surrenders to the loving embrace of God as a bride to her bridegroom. These are the "Beloved Ones of God," men and women madly in love and burning to know Him ever more deeply, to love Her ever more fully. They are lovers who have heard the divine love song and sing back, harmonizing with Divinity. Knowing God, as Love, Lover, and Beloved, opens oneself wholly and completely to the Divine. God is felt as a deep unity and love for all of humanity.

Romancing the Beloved: Time with the Beloved

Mystics are not dreamy believers out of touch with reality; they, in fact, are the ones potentially in touch with Reality.

"My friend signed me up to do a Buddhist retreat. It was eight days in the silence. In thirty-one years I had never stopped talking. I was panicked! Everything was done as a meditation: sitting, walking, and eating. There were at least a hundred people doing the retreat with me, together and yet completely and

individually absorbed. My state of awareness was completely altered. I was seeing, hearing, sensing, and discovering the earth in all her beauty, as if for the very first time. In the mornings, I had kitchen duty and had to get up before the crack of dawn to help prepare breakfast. On my way to the kitchen a big black bear came galloping along beside me, traveling with me in the deep green grass along the same path. Inside the silence, my soul was frolicking."

Retreats are exclusive times set aside to romance the Beloved. They are held in private or in the presence of a spiritual community. For deepening and silence, spiritual retreats are secure environments, located in remote settings surrounded by the natural world, such as cabins in the mountains, bungalows on a beach, or the sanctity of a private home.

"Every day I wake and sing a song of praise. I light a candle and burn some incense. Then I go to the parlor and meditate. I go outside and greet the sun, journal, and reflect on my dreams. I go for a walk and take in the awesome beauty of the planet as I listen to the birds sing, watch flowers blossom, raindrops dance, snowflakes sail, leaves fall from trees and do the rustle, all the while in the sound of silence. Sometimes I extend my week-day practices into entire weekends."

Deep listening is the act of attending to the call of the Beloved, a time for re-evaluation and re-visioning, living in and responding to the question. Romancing the Beloved is a conscious pause, patience in the stillness, rest and tranquility reverberating in states of reverie. Inhalation and inspiration, with exaltation expressing itself on the breath of voicelessness, the sweet lyrics of poesies — images to words, symbols and dreams reveling with desire and evolving into continuous prayer, days on end with the Beloved. Out of nothingness comes the taste of the "wine of ecstasy" in the One fully embodied.

"I signed up for a ten day retreat with the Dances of Universal Peace to celebrate and pray on behalf of the Earth. I had been searching for spiritual venues that would offer me a fully conscious experience of the Divine while being in the body. At the first session, nearly a hundred people started walking in a circle, breathing together, feeling the earth, the bones of our ancestors beneath the soles of our bare feet. A beautiful dance leader in the image of a divine goddess began playing her guitar and singing a song, and instantly I recollected a dream — the dream now unfolding before my eyes, as the goddess sang offering chants of blessing, as she spiraled the group into a great circle holding each other's hands. It was pure ecstasy

with my eyes open while my body animated this prayer. I was completely transported. All day and into the night we danced and sang sacred songs and mantras from all the religions of the world, deepening the unity, creating love, harmony, and beauty. I had remembered my friends and discovered my path."

This incredible place is the result of continuous prayer. One is free to participate in a love affair, an endless banquet of soul-making. In the vicinity of the Beloved, one enters the place of remembrance, like a return journey when you're going home. In Her periphery, the Beloved bestows a sense of refinement and grace. Spiritual practice polishes the rust from the heart and elicits a transitory reprieve from disturbance. Presence with the Beloved is timeless, eternal, and never-ending. Love pervades and beauty prevails. It is the direct experience of the perfect love, an ever-love.

There are many paths to God. On the mystical path of love, as we enter a courtship with the ultimate reality, life begins to exemplify such characteristics as inclusiveness, complexity, and interrelatedness. Mystical relatedness softens the boundaries — that hard separateness of I, me, and mine — and links us with the collective in consciousness, the expression of divine love in the world. The world needs our love.

The Path of Love

What is it like to experience heaven on earth? It is waking up in the manifestation of everything you have prayed for and everything you have dreamed. There is this sense of being cared for and taken care of, rather than having to care for and take care of. "Even though I am making the chicken soup, the chicken soup is being made for me." There is an organic continuum of provision, support, and love which nurtures and nourishes the soul. I remember my innocence. Heaven is near, the expression of complete balance, a steady heartbeat pulses through my system. Without a doubt, I know that I am completely and totally loved. Absorbed in love, it is pure bliss, the ecstasy of heaven here on earth. My body and consciousness serve as a divine temple, animating love in the world. It is the fruit blossoming from my vine entwined with the One: intuition, prophecy, divine intervention, manifestation. The world is a magical kingdom.

The feeling I have today... I notice a certain kind of pulse. I hear a love song singing from my heart. I know true love and it is delicious. In this place there is no hunger. Here there is Love.

God is my Yenta

"One day I was walking around the block and asked the Beloved, 'Who should I love?' No response. The next day and day after I would ask the beloved, 'Who do I love?' No answer. As the months passed, I continued to ask, adding things like, 'I really want to be with someone who is my equal, an individual.' Days went on — 'Someone who is clean and pure.' And so on — 'I would especially like to be with someone who can respect my love for the spiritual life.'

Nearly a year had passed as I continued to listen and pray for guidance. On an early spring day I asked once again, 'Beloved, who do you want me to love?' And finally I heard, 'Love Ahad!' I said 'Ahad? Who is Ahad?' and God said, 'He is the One.'

"I thought, 'Oh, Ahad — the guy in Santa Fe who lives like a monk.' And then suddenly it hit me and I said, 'Oh, my God, he is the one! I just love Ahad!'"

The Path of Love

Ahad writes:

"I had been celibate, without a lover, for fourteen years. I had finally given up on hoping and wishing and longing and projecting my unfulfilled desire. I had dedicated myself to the ideal of transpersonal love and service to humanity. I was self-contained and only lonely some of the time. Until I met you.... who were so beautiful, so spiritual, who expressed such love for me that I experienced heavens of light opening up above me.

"My soul was attracted but still cautious. Then one night we were sitting across the room conversing with each other. Suddenly the image of my first beloved floated in front of your face, the image of true love right here and now, and I felt the rusty cage around my heart, a cage I had not known was there, it creaked as the door opened, and I very clearly heard the words, 'The path of love.'

"That was it. This is the path of love.

"We kept our love very private for many months, this newborn held closely between us. When I finally told my oldest friend that I was in love, she said, 'I am so happy for you! Just remember — you must never stop courting her!'"

Afterword

In many traditional societies marriages are arranged by the families to insure continuity of bloodline, social status, and wealth, and hopefully happiness for the young couple. In the medieval society "with parental permission it was legal for boys to marry at fourteen and girls at twelve. A betrothal often took place when the prospective bride and groom were as young as seven years old and in the case of higher nobility many were betrothed as babies." Arranged marriages are common in Arab, Hindu, and many other societies to this day. The valued role of matchmaker is filled by priests, rabbis, and astrologers, who serve as go-betweens for the two families, saving the bride and groom the embarrassment of having to meet before they are fully approved by the parents, the stars, and God. Needless to say the ideals of courtly love and romance operated totally apart from the social conventions of arranged marriage.

In the twenty-first century, our courtship landscape is expanded and complicated by modern technology, by texting and sexting, by social networks such as Facebook, by online dating services, not to mention international mail-order brides and bridegrooms. Tens of millions of people have virtual relationships, romantic and otherwise, with tens of millions of other people they may never meet face to face. Millions of people look for marriage partners on line, while millions more look for casual sex hook ups. While the shadow of internet dating may be consumerism, impersonality, and "ironic detachment," the promise is greater access to compatible partners in today's chaotic society.

With the advent of internet dating, cyber matchmaking has gained momentum as the modern day matchmaker through sites such as eHarmony or Match.com. The desire to experience romantic love and the pursuit of happiness has given birth to an overwhelming number of internet marriages. It is claimed that approximately one in every six marriages today are the result of internet dating systems. Technology is the charm for happiness. The search for happiness is founded on elaborate personality, brain chemistry, and genetic compatibility tests, which are geared to maximize the best possible match. No matter how vast the modern social landscape, the heart still beats in the breast, and the lover is still looking for the beloved, without and within. We never want to forget to rely on feelings, intuition, and a good sense of smell.

Definitions

The **psyche** holds the totality of our mental functioning, both conscious as well as unconscious. Our conscious function involves awareness of one's environment and one's own existence, sensations, and thoughts. The unconscious function is the dimension of the psyche which possesses continuous change, force, and vigor. The unconscious cannot be scientifically proven, only experientially inferred from its manifestations in dreams, symbols, behaviors, and symptoms.

A **symptom** is defined as a way of remembering something necessary not to forget or forgetting something which at the moment is too painful to remember. Symptoms are personal, cultural, and ecological. Illness and disease are part of the disconnection. Symptoms also surface as symbolic manifestations in a person's life, i.e., chronic pain in one's heart, dreaming wars, swine flu disease, obesity, and so on. Symptoms are the voice of the World Soul. Our personal life becomes grafted onto the collective history of humanity, and that collective history becomes grafted onto our personal life.

Attending to one's mental health is achieved in the course of individual development between conscious and unconscious processes. The work of individuation is to make the unconscious conscious, thereby liberating ourselves from emotional states and patterns which are debilitating to emotional maturity.

The **ego** is the focal point of consciousness — "I" or "me". It is the conscious organizer of our thoughts and intuitions, our feelings and sensations. It has access to those memories which are unrepressed and readily available. The ego is a mediator of Self to the world and world to the Self. The Self is the center but also the circumference which embraces both consciousness and unconsciousness. The Self is at the center of this totality, just as the ego is at the center of the conscious mind. The model of the ego is separation, while the model of the Self is inclusive.

The **Self** is the dominant archetype whereby the development of the personality successfully culminates in the expression of individuation. An individual becomes as complete a human being as possible. When there is no dialogue or inquiry between the ego and the Self, the ego remains limited and run by the forces of the unconscious. Pain and suffering between self and other creates and re-creates patterns of symptoms and behaviors activated by our complexes.

A **complex** is a group of associated ideas bound together by a shared emotional charge; it exerts a dynamic effect on conscious experience and behavior. For example, some people suffer from an abandonment complex: with every intimate relationship they enact and reenact dramas which reinforce abandonment complexities. Many people will experience one form or another of the father or mother complex. One will tend to react to any caregiver or authority figure that triggers the symptoms which had previously been accrued by adapting to the father or mother. One will tend to behave toward those figures with the same set of coping skills one learned as a result of the original wound.

Complexes seem to possess a will, a life, and a personality of their own, which can be functionally healthy and/or unhealthy. At the heart of a complex there is a nuclear element which functions beyond the reach of the conscious will. Around this nucleus emotionally charged ideas and associations cluster. When these ideas and associations are triggered through interactions with others, the complex is activated. An example of a healthy functional complex would be inner security, which promotes esteem, confidence, and a realistic self identity. A healthy, secure person can interface with the world and remain emotionally stable.

Sources and Citations

Chapter One: Courtly Love

Bailey, Beth, *From Front Porch To Backseat: Courtship in Twentieth-Century America* (Baltimore and London: The John Hopkins University Press, 1988).

http://en.wikipedia.org/wiki/Troubadour
http://en.wikipedia.org/wiki/Courtly_love
http://condor.depaul.edu/~dsimpson/tlove/courtlylove.html
http://www.wsu.edu/~delahoyd/medieval/love.html
http://www.cs.utk.edu/~mclennan/Classes/US310/Interp-Court-Love.html
http://www.cs.utk.edu/~mclennan/Classes/US310/Dante-Fedeli-d-Amore.html
http://www.umanista.net/uk/fedeli.html

p. 12 *"To seek to gain or achieve..."*: http://mw4.m-w.com/dictionary/courting

Chapter Two: Personal Mythology

Bolen, Jean Shinoda, *Gods In Every Man: A New Psychology of Men's Lives & Loves* (New York: Harper & Row, 1989).

Cloninger, Susan, *Theories of Personality: Understanding Persons*, Third Ed. (New Jersey: Prentice Hall, 2000).

Hillman, James, *Healing Fiction* (Woodstock Connecticut: Spring Publications, 1983).

Houston, Jean, *The Search for the Beloved: Journeys in Mythology & Sacred Psychology* (New York: Tarcher /Putnam, 1987).

Papillon, Lucy, *When Hope Can Kill: Reclaiming Your Soul In A Romantic Relationship* (Tennessee: Everywhere Press, 1998).

Stevens, Anthony, *On Jung* (New York: Penguin Books, 1990).

Zweig, Connie, *The Holy Longing: The Hidden Power of Spiritual Yearning* (New York: Tarcher/ Putnam, 2003).

http://en.wikipedia.org/wiki/Cupid_and_Psyche

http://www.paleothea.com/Myths/Psyche.html

http://webspace.ship.edu/cgboer/psyche.html

http://thanasis.com/echo.htm

p. 35 You can't change early life experiences....: Susan Nettleton, *Self-Esteem*, from an unpublished lecture at the Hillside Community Church (Albuquerque, NM, 2000).

p. 36 How do you know who you are?....: Ibid.

Chapter Three: Soul Mates: A Myth that Splits

Cowan, Lyn, *Portrait of the Blue Lady: The Character of Melancholy* (New Orleans: Louisiana, 2004).

Plato, *The Symposium*, translated by W. Hamilton (New York: Penguin, 1951).

Turner, Victor, *Betwixt and Between: The Liminal Period in Rites of Passage* (La Salle, Illinois: Open Court, 1987).

Vaughn, C., *How Life Begins: The Science of Life in the Womb* (New York: Random House, 1996).

http://en.wikipedia.org/wiki/Soulmate

http://en.wikipedia.org/wiki/Androgyny

http://en.wikipedia.org/wiki/Postgenderism

http://en.wikipedia.org/wiki/Gender

http://www.sinauer.com/levay3e/sample/LeVay3e_Ch06_Instructors_ Manual.doc
http://www.narth.com/docs/berman2.html

p. 43 "controlled by our parents…": *Wagoner's Lad*, Traditional folk song

p. 44 "Lovers don't finally meet…": Coleman, Barks, *The Essential Rumi* (San Francisco: Harper, 1995), p.106.

Chapter Four: Sexual History

Davies, Nigel, *The Rampant God* (New York: William Morrow, 1984).
Fisher, Helen, *Anatomy of Love: A Natural History of Mating, Marriage, and Why we Stray* (New York: Fawcett Columbine, 1992).

p. 55 "just as the male and female aspects…" http://spiritualsensuality. blogspot.com/2006/11/sabbath-sex.htm
l

Chapter Five: The Biology and Chemistry of Love

Fisher, Helen, *Why We Love: The Nature And Chemistry of Romantic Love* (New York: Henry Holt and Company, 2004).
Fisher, Helen, *Lust, Romance, Attachment: The Drive to Love*, from an unpublished lecture at The Self and Family conference (Santa Fe NM, 2010).
Fisher, Helen, *Why Him? Why Her? How Your Biological Temperament Steers Why You Will Love and How You Love*, from an unpublished lecture at The Self and Family conference (Santa Fe NM, 2010).
Morris, Desmond, *Intimate Behaviour* (New York: Random House, 1971).

http://en.wikipedia.org/wiki/Pheromone
http://www.webmd.com/sex-relationships/features/sex-life-phermones
http://www.livescience.com/health/090114-human-pheromones.html

http://www.athenainstitute.com/ispne.html
http://en.wikipedia.org/wiki/Limbic_system\
http://en.wikipedia.org/wiki/Helen_Fisher_(anthropologist)
http://www.mcmanweb.com/love_lust.html
http://people.howstuffworks.com/love.htm
http://www.romancestuck.com/articles/chemistryoflove.htm
http://www.livingonearth.org/shows/segments.htm?programID=08-P13-00006&segmentID=8
http://www.helenfisher.com/downloads/articles/14defining.pdf

Chapter Six: Love in the Twenty-first Century: Alternative Models and Trends

Coontz, Stephanie, *Marriage, a History: from Obedience to Intimacy or How Love Conquered Marriage* (New York: Penguin, 2005).

Fonagy, Peter, *Attachment Theory and Psychoanalysis* (New York: Guilford Press, 1999).

Khan, Hazrat Inayat, *The Sufi Message of Hazrat Inayat Kahn, Vol. 6. Rasa Shastra* (Geneva: Barrie & Rockliff, 1960)

Loh, Sandra Tsing, *The case against marriage*, The Week, Vol. 9, Issue 421 (2009).

p. 77 Human love promises to initiate us…: Zweig, Connie, *The Holy Longing: The Hidden Power of Spiritual Yearning* (New York: Putnam Press, 2003), p.79

p. 77 A window onto the divine…: Ibid., p.89

p. 82 Just because it is our experience…: Waterman, Robert, *Evolution of Consciousness*, from an unpublished lecture at Southwestern College (Santa Fe, New Mexico, 1986).

p. 89 In order for romantic involvements…: *Mitchell, Stephen, Can Love Last? The Fate Of Romance Over Time* (New York: Norton, 2002), p.199.

p. 93 Thy Light in all forms…: Kahn, Hazrat Inayat, *The Sufi Message of Hazrat Inayat Kahn: Gayan, Vadan, Nirtan* (London: Barrie and Jenkins, 1960), p.76.

p. 93 Spell of the sensuous: Abram, David, *The Spell of the Sensuous* (New York: Vintage, 1996).

p. 93 Who makes love…: Douglas-Klotz, Neil, from an unpublished lecture at a retreat at Lama Foundation (Taos, New Mexico, 1999).

p. 96 The earthly with the universal spirit…: Sardello, Robert, *Love And The Soul: Creating a Future for Earth* (New York: Harper Collins, 1995), p.44.

p. 96 recollection of the whole of the creation…: Ibid., p. 51

p. 97 Marriage revolution: Fisher, Helen, *Why Him? Why Her? How your Biological Temperament Steers Why You Will Love and How You Love*, from an unpublished lecture at The Self and Family conference (Santa Fe NM, 2010).

p. 97 perfected carries the attributes…: Khan, Hazrat Inayat, *The Sufi Message of Hazrat Inayat Khan, Vol. 3* (Geneva: Barrie & Rockliff, 1960), p. 122.

p. 98 ray of light…: Ibid., p.127.

p. 100 stimulate each partner to progress…: Ibid., p.156.

p. 101 For the joy and devotion…: Ibid., p.172.

p. 101 The thing about friends…: Pir Shabda, Kahn, *Pir Shabda Kahn & Friends Live In Boston 2003: The Music of Life Retreat* (Boston Mass. 2003), track 13.

Chapter Seven: Love and The Erotic Pulse

Bennett, Mary Rose, *Blood Psyche: Body, Ancestry, and Soul*, Pacifica Graduate Institute, (Santa Barbara, CA, 2001), pp.56-60.

Ramsay, Jay, Alchemy: *The Art of Transformation*, (London: Harper Collins 1997).

p. 103 The field of desire...: Marlan, Stan, *Fire In The Stone: The Alchemy of Desire* (Wilmette: IL., 1997), p.14.

p. 104 Psychologically, we might say...: Zweig, Connie, T*he Holy Longing: The Hidden Power of Spiritual Yearning* (New York: Putnam Press, 2003), p./4.

Chapter Eight: The Inner Turn: The Eternal Courtship

p. 109 Spiritual attainment...: Khan, Hazrat Inayat, *The Sufi Message of Hazrat Inayat Kahn, Vol. 2* (Great Britain: Camelot Press, 1960), p.147.

p. 110 The study of the self...: Ibid., p.126

p. 111 Psychological gnosis...: Romanyshyn, Robert, *Psychological Studies*, from an unpublished lecture at Pacifica Graduate Institute (Santa Barbara, CA, 1996).

p. 112 We are in a field of flesh...: Ibid.

p. 112 the royal road...: Cloninger, Susan, *Theories of Personality: Understanding Persons*. Third Edition (New Jersey: Prentice Hall, 2000), p.40.

p. 112 In the dream it is not only imagination…: Khan, Hazrat Inayat, *The Sufi Message of Hazrat Inayat Kahn, Vol. 2* (Great Britain: Camelot Press, 1960), p.256.

p. 114 By devotion, heaven…: Khan, Hazrat Inayat, *The Sufi Message of Hazrat Inayat Kahn, Vol. 7* (Great Britain: Camelot Press, 1962), p.265.

p. 115 in communion with all beings…: Khan, Hazrat Inayat, *The Sufi Message of Hazrat Inayat Kahn, Vol. 2* (Great Britain: Camelot Press, 1960), p.133.

Chapter Nine: The Path of the Mystic

Harvey, Andrew and Hanut, Eryk, *Perfume of the Desert, Inspirations from Sufi Wisdom*, Wheaton, IL: Quest Books, 1999

Underhill, Evelyn. *Mysticism: The Preeminent Study In The Nature And Development of Spiritual Consciousness.* New York: Doubleday, 1990.

http: // en.wikipedia.org/wiki/Mysticism

p. 118 Meister Eckhart, Rabbi Herschel quotes: Zweig, Connie, *The Holy Longing: The Hidden Power of Spiritual Yearning* (New York: Putnam Press, 2003), p.23.

p. 118 becomes conscious of one's own self…: Khan, Hazrat Inayat, *The Heart of Sufism: Essential Writings of Hazrat Inayat Khan* (Boston: Shambhala, 1999), p.232.

p. 119 the Beloved, the only Beloved there is…: Khan, Hazrat Inayat, *The Heart of Sufism: Essential Writings of Hazrat Inayat Khan* (Boston, Massachusetts: Shambhala, 1999), p. 245.

p. 119 The Hindustani poet...: Khan, Hazrat Inayat, *The Sufi Message of Hazrat Inayat Khan, Vol. 3* (Geneva: Barrie & Rockliff, 1960), p. 122.

p. 120 only the love of God can fulfill...: Khan, Hazrat Inayat, *Song of the Prophets: The Unity of Religious Ideals* (New Lebanon, NY: Omega, 2009), p. 49.

Afterword

http://www.onlinedatingmagazine.com/mediacenter/onlinedatingfacts.html
http:// connections.afroromance.com/Dating Advice/68/view/online-dating-is-everybody-really-doing-it/
http:// www.syl.com/singles/datingstatistics.html
http:// gracechopper.org/2008/assets/algorithms of love poster. pdf
http:// ezinearticles.com/ A-Glimpse-at-Online-Dating-Statistics &id = 14444358
http:// www.en.wikipedia.org/wiki/Matchmaking
http://www.en. wikikipedia.org/wiki/ Yenta

p. 130 with parental permission it was legal....:http://www.middle-ages. org.uk/noble-women-in-the-middle-ages.htm